API gateway design patterns for cloud computing

The Ultimate Guide to Orchestrating APIs, Securing
Microservices, and Powering Scalable Cloud System

SIMON TELLIER

Table of Contents

Preface

Why This Book Was Written

Modern software systems are no longer confined to single, self-contained monoliths. Today's applications are dynamic networks of microservices, APIs, serverless functions, legacy integrations, and cloud-native components that must work together in real time. In such distributed environments, the API gateway has emerged as a critical architectural cornerstone — serving as the entry point, the policy enforcer, the traffic cop, and the translator between consumers and backend services.

Yet, despite the growing reliance on API gateways in cloud computing, many development teams still struggle with effectively designing, implementing, and managing them. Most online materials are scattered, shallow, or heavily biased toward specific vendor implementations. Architecture books tend to gloss over the operational complexities, while product documentation rarely offers context for real-world decisions across diverse infrastructures.

This book was written to bridge that gap — to provide not just a reference, but a practical guide for designing and implementing effective API gateway architectures in the cloud. Whether you're building a new platform from scratch, modernizing a legacy stack, or scaling APIs to serve millions of requests, this book equips you with the patterns, tools, and proven techniques to get it right.

It reflects the author's years of experience designing distributed systems, working with DevOps teams on deployment automation, collaborating with enterprise architects on security strategies, and navigating the real challenges that come with managing APIs in production. This book is a consolidation of field-tested practices, vendor-agnostic patterns, and deployment know-how tailored to what actually works — not just what looks good on paper.

At its core, this book is about helping engineers and architects build more reliable, secure, and scalable cloud platforms using API gateways as a foundational layer. It's about understanding not only how gateways function, but when, where, and why to use them. And it's about making design decisions confidently, with clarity and foresight.

That's why this book was written — to empower you with practical architecture wisdom in a fast-changing cloud world.

Who This Book Is For

This book was written with several key audiences in mind. While their job titles may vary, they all face similar challenges in managing distributed systems, securing APIs, and ensuring seamless access to cloud services.

1. Cloud Architects

If you're designing multi-region or multi-cloud platforms, you understand that proper gateway placement and design can make or break your system's performance, reliability, and security posture. This book offers high-level strategy as well as implementation details to support your architectural decisions.

2. DevOps Engineers and Platform Teams

You are responsible for keeping systems running smoothly, automating deployments, and ensuring observability. You'll find actionable advice for integrating gateways into CI/CD pipelines, setting up proper logging, implementing health checks, and avoiding misconfigurations that can lead to outages.

3. Backend Developers and API Designers

For developers, understanding how APIs are consumed, transformed, throttled, and secured at the gateway layer is essential. This book demystifies the "black box" of gateway behavior, helping you design APIs that are gateway-friendly and performant across environments.

4. Security Engineers

If you're focused on API authentication, authorization, token validation, or rate-limiting, this book will give you practical guidance on securing cloud-native APIs using modern identity and access management strategies. It dives into patterns like Zero Trust, JWT validation, and OAuth2 flows across popular gateways.

5. Technical Product Managers and Engineering Leads

This book is also for leaders who are steering technical direction and need a deeper understanding of how gateways fit into the bigger system picture. If you're responsible for roadmap alignment, vendor evaluations, or SLA compliance, the strategic patterns and real-world examples included here will give you clarity and confidence.

Whether you're operating in a startup, a government agency, or a large enterprise, if your systems rely on APIs — and especially if you're navigating a microservices or hybrid cloud architecture — this book is for you.

How to Use This Book

This book is designed to be both a cover-to-cover guide and a reference manual you can revisit whenever you face a gateway-related design decision or implementation challenge.

Here's how to get the most value from it:

1. Read Part I First, Regardless of Your Role

The foundational chapters explain why gateways matter, how they evolved, and the architectural principles that underpin them. This section sets the stage for everything that follows. Even if you're an experienced practitioner, revisiting these concepts in a structured way will help unify your mental model before diving into more advanced material.

2. Use the Patterns in Part II as Your Design Toolbox

Each chapter in Part II presents a well-established gateway design pattern, including detailed explanations, practical use cases, trade-offs, and real-world implementation examples. These are intended to be modular — you can read and apply them independently based on the problems you're solving.

3. Dive Into Cloud-Specific Chapters as Needed

Part III dives deep into gateway implementations across AWS, Azure, GCP, Kong, and NGINX, among others. Use these chapters to understand how core patterns translate into specific services and platforms. If you're working in a multi-cloud or hybrid environment, these comparisons will help you identify the best tools for each job.

4. Bookmark the Security and CI/CD Chapters in Part IV

Security and automation are non-negotiable in modern API systems. Part IV offers clear, practical solutions for handling authentication, observability, deployment, and resilience.

These chapters are rich with checklists, example pipelines, and production-hardened practices.

5. Leverage Part V for Advanced Scaling and Multi-Tenancy

When your platform grows in complexity or user base, you'll face problems that require more than just basic gateway configurations. Part V addresses these scenarios with detailed discussions on multi-tenancy, hybrid cloud patterns, dynamic routing, and scaling for millions of requests per minute.

6. Use the Appendices and Glossary for Quick Access

In the final section, you'll find:

- A comparison matrix of popular gateways

- Infrastructure-as-code templates

- OpenAPI integration strategies

- Checklists for securing and launching gateways

- A glossary for quick explanations of key terms and acronyms

These resources are practical and copy-paste ready — designed to make your job easier, not harder.

In short: whether you're trying to architect, secure, debug, or scale your API infrastructure, this book provides a reliable, well-structured path forward. You don't need to read it all in one go — but it's here whenever you're ready for the next step in your cloud API journey.

Companion GitHub Repository and Resources

To ensure that the lessons in this book are not only conceptual but also immediately applicable, we've provided a full set of practical resources hosted in a companion GitHub repository.

Here's what you'll find inside:

■ Design Pattern Implementations

Each core design pattern — from the Edge Gateway to BFF to Aggregator — is accompanied by:

- YAML configurations

- Terraform scripts

- NGINX/Kong plugin examples

- Code samples in Node.js, Go, and Python

These examples are written to reflect real-world production readiness, not just demos.

■ CI/CD Pipeline Templates

You'll find GitHub Actions, GitLab CI/CD pipelines, and Docker Compose samples for:

- Deploying gateway configurations

- Running integration tests

- Rolling out blue-green or canary deployments

These templates align with the practices described in Part IV and are ready to adapt for your own needs.

■ OpenAPI/Swagger Integration Files

Example specifications and automation scripts to:

- Generate gateway configurations from OpenAPI specs

- Validate spec changes via CI

- Version and deploy updated APIs safely

■ Kubernetes and Service Mesh Integration Examples

Sample manifests and Istio Gateway configurations to help bridge the gap between Kubernetes-native systems and gateway-layer designs.

■ Visual Diagrams and Architecture Flows

All diagrams presented in the book (and more) are available in downloadable formats — ideal for including in your documentation, architecture reviews, or internal slide decks.

■ Debugging and Troubleshooting Recipes

Step-by-step instructions for solving common issues like:

- Authentication failures

- Routing misconfigurations

- Latency and caching problems

- Cross-origin (CORS) errors

Repository Access

A link to the companion repository and all access instructions are included at the start of Chapter 1. The repo will be actively maintained and updated based on reader feedback and evolving technology trends.

If you find a pattern especially helpful — or you've improved on it — we welcome contributions from the community. You're not just reading a book; you're joining a growing network of API builders, architects, and defenders working to make cloud systems better, safer, and more scalable.

Now that you know the "why", "who", and "how" behind this book, it's time to begin exploring the powerful world of API gateway design patterns — and build systems ready for the demands of today's cloud-first future.

PART I — Foundations of API Gateways in the Cloud

Before diving into specific patterns and implementations, it's essential to build a clear and practical understanding of what API gateways are, why they matter, and how they fit into modern cloud architecture. Part I lays this groundwork.

This section traces the evolution of the API gateway, from its early role as a simple traffic router to its current status as a vital control plane for managing microservices, securing APIs, and orchestrating access across complex distributed environments.

You'll explore how API gateways differ from traditional proxies, how they relate to service meshes, and what deployment models exist in today's cloud-native and hybrid infrastructures. Whether you're new to the concept or looking to refine your architectural approach, Part I equips you with the conceptual clarity and architectural context needed to understand — and use — API gateways effectively.

By the end of this part, you'll have the foundation required to confidently design and evaluate gateway strategies across platforms like AWS, Azure, GCP, and open-source solutions like Kong and NGINX.

Chapter 1: The Role of API Gateways in Modern Cloud Architectures

1.1 What is an API Gateway?

In the past, software systems often operated as tightly coupled monoliths. All components lived under the same roof — data access, business logic, user interfaces — and there was no need for sophisticated intermediaries to manage communication. But as applications evolved toward service-oriented and, eventually, microservice-based designs, that architectural simplicity was replaced by highly distributed systems.

In this new world of hundreds — even thousands — of independently deployed services, API gateways emerged out of necessity. An API gateway is a server or service that acts as a single entry point for external or internal clients to access backend services. It sits at the front of your infrastructure, intercepting incoming API requests, routing them to the appropriate microservices, applying policies, and handling the responses.

But a gateway is much more than just a router. It functions as a traffic controller, security enforcer, rate limiter, protocol translator, and observability hook — all rolled into one. It abstracts the complexity of backend services and provides a unified interface to the outside world.

At its core, the API gateway addresses several key challenges in cloud-native development:

- Service discovery: Knowing where services are and how to reach them.

- Security: Validating tokens, controlling access, encrypting data in transit.

- Protocol management: Translating between HTTP, WebSocket, gRPC, and legacy protocols.

- Request shaping: Transforming incoming requests or outgoing responses to match API contracts.

- Rate limiting and throttling: Preventing abuse or accidental overload of backend services.

In essence, an API gateway acts as the public face of your microservice ecosystem — streamlining external access while protecting and optimizing internal service communication.

1.2 API Gateway vs Load Balancer vs Reverse Proxy

These terms often come up in the same conversation, but they serve very different roles — and understanding the distinction is critical when architecting distributed systems.

Load Balancer

A load balancer distributes incoming network or application traffic across multiple servers or instances to ensure high availability and reliability. It operates at Layer 4 (TCP/UDP) or Layer 7 (HTTP/HTTPS), depending on the setup. Load balancers do not typically modify request content or perform access control. Their job is to keep traffic moving efficiently.

Think of a load balancer as a bouncer at a nightclub — it doesn't care who you are, just that you go into the next available room with enough space.

Reverse Proxy

A reverse proxy is a server that sits between clients and backend servers, forwarding client requests to appropriate servers and returning the server's response back to the client. While similar to a load balancer, a reverse proxy can perform more advanced Layer 7 actions like header modification, URL rewriting, or caching.

A reverse proxy is like a concierge — it can direct you, explain rules, and even repackage things before passing them along.

API Gateway

An API gateway is a specialized type of reverse proxy that focuses specifically on managing and securing API calls. While it may include load balancing or proxying functionality, its real value lies in its ability to:

- Authenticate and authorize requests

- Apply rate limiting and usage quotas

- Handle API versioning

- Translate protocols

- Log and trace calls for observability

An API gateway is more like a high-security, full-service receptionist — checking credentials, deciding if you're allowed in, keeping a log, and sending alerts if something suspicious happens.

12

In short:

Feature	Load Balancer	Reverse Proxy	API Gateway
Traffic Routing	☑	☑	☑
Protocol Translation	✖	☑	☑
Authentication	✖	⚠ (limited)	☑
Rate Limiting	✖	✖	☑
API Versioning	✖	✖	☑
Logging & Tracing	⚠	⚠	☑
Developer Portal	✖	✖	☑

While reverse proxies and load balancers are essential in networking infrastructure, only the API gateway provides the full range of capabilities needed to manage APIs effectively in the cloud.

1.3 Centralization of API Traffic

One of the most powerful outcomes of adopting an API gateway is the centralization of API traffic. In a microservices environment, individual services are typically decoupled, independently deployed, and may expose their own endpoints. Without a centralized layer, API management becomes chaotic — security rules are inconsistent, observability is fragmented, and changes require coordination across multiple teams.

The API gateway acts as a unified control plane, consolidating access across all services. This centralization brings several important advantages:

1. Security Policies at the Edge

By enforcing authentication, authorization, and encryption policies at the gateway, you avoid duplicating security logic inside every microservice. Token validation, IP restrictions, and CORS rules can all be handled uniformly at the edge.

2. Simplified Client Interactions

Instead of clients needing to know the locations, protocols, and API signatures of dozens of backend services, they interact with a single URL — the gateway. The gateway then handles routing and response transformation behind the scenes.

3. Operational Visibility

Centralization enables complete logging and tracing of requests. If something fails, you can quickly pinpoint whether it was the client, the gateway, or the backend service — a major advantage for SRE and DevOps teams.

4. Version and Traffic Management

With centralized traffic, it's easy to roll out new API versions using path-based routing, header flags, or weighted distributions — enabling canary deployments, blue/green releases, or feature toggling without needing to redeploy everything at once.

Of course, centralization must be designed with resilience and redundancy in mind — a single chokepoint can quickly become a system-wide failure if not handled properly. We'll cover high availability design later in the book. For now, understand that centralizing API traffic isn't just a technical convenience — it's an operational and strategic advantage in managing cloud-native systems.

1.4 When and Why You Need an API Gateway

Not every system starts out needing an API gateway. But once your architecture begins to scale, the need becomes unmistakable. Let's explore the conditions under which an API gateway becomes essential — and why.

■ You Have Multiple Microservices or Backend APIs

Managing APIs independently across teams leads to inconsistency and increased security risks. A gateway consolidates entry points, enforces standards, and prevents configuration drift.

■ You Need Consistent Security Across Services

Implementing token validation or OAuth flows inside every microservice is not only inefficient, it's dangerous. An API gateway centralizes security enforcement and ensures policies are uniformly applied.

■ You Want to Expose APIs to External Clients

If your application offers public APIs to partners, mobile apps, or third-party integrators, a gateway acts as a buffer — enforcing quotas, shaping traffic, and protecting against misuse.

■ You're Using Serverless or Cloud-Native Services

In serverless environments like AWS Lambda or Azure Functions, gateways are almost always required to manage RESTful access, authenticate users, and aggregate logic across functions.

■ You Need Monitoring, Auditing, and Tracing

API gateways provide a central point for capturing logs, metrics, and distributed tracing data. This is invaluable for debugging, compliance, and performance tuning.

■ You're Managing Legacy APIs Alongside Modern Ones

Gateways can abstract away protocol differences and expose a unified RESTful interface to clients — even if the backend services are SOAP, RPC, or on-premise mainframes.

■ You Want to Support API Versioning and Developer Onboarding

Gateways often integrate with developer portals that provide documentation, test consoles, and API keys — streamlining onboarding and lifecycle management.

■ You Need to Rate Limit or Monetize API Usage

Whether to prevent abuse or implement tiered billing, gateways offer fine-grained quota management per user, key, or IP.

If any of these scenarios apply to your system — and in cloud-native environments, they usually do — an API gateway is not a luxury; it's a necessity.

1.5 Common Use Cases in Cloud-Native Ecosystems

Let's explore some of the most common and impactful use cases where API gateways prove indispensable in modern cloud-based systems.

1. Edge Authentication for Public APIs

A SaaS platform offering public APIs uses a gateway to authenticate users via OAuth2, validate tokens, and forward only authorized requests to backend services. This keeps authentication logic centralized and reduces the attack surface of core services.

2. Mobile and IoT Backend Aggregation

A mobile application hits a single gateway endpoint that aggregates data from five microservices — user profile, device status, notifications, billing, and analytics. The gateway combines these responses into a single payload, reducing the number of round-trips and improving app performance.

3. Legacy System Wrapping

An enterprise integrates an old on-prem SAP system that exposes SOAP APIs. The gateway wraps these APIs into RESTful endpoints, enabling modern frontends and partner integrations without requiring changes to the legacy system.

4. Serverless Orchestration

A cloud-native startup builds its backend on AWS Lambda. API Gateway becomes the public interface for all endpoints, handling path routing, CORS, and request validation. It also supports usage plans to throttle API calls based on paid tiers.

5. Rate Limiting and Abuse Protection

A fintech company offering market data APIs uses a gateway to enforce per-user rate limits, prevent scraping, and throttle high-volume requests to maintain stability during peak market hours.

6. Multi-Tenant Routing

A B2B platform hosts services for multiple clients. The API gateway inspects tokens or request headers to determine the tenant, routes traffic accordingly, and applies tenant-specific quotas or policies.

7. API Versioning and Traffic Shaping

During a major backend refactor, the engineering team supports /v1 and /v2 API versions side-by-side. The gateway routes traffic based on the URL path, enabling a smooth migration while supporting legacy clients.

8. Cross-Origin Resource Sharing (CORS) Management

Instead of configuring CORS headers in every backend microservice, the gateway centrally manages allowed origins, headers, and methods — simplifying policy enforcement across environments.

9. Logging and Monitoring for Compliance

In a regulated industry like healthcare or finance, capturing API access logs and audit trails is critical. The gateway provides centralized, tamper-proof logging and integrates with monitoring tools like Prometheus, CloudWatch, or Azure Monitor.

These are not hypothetical scenarios — they reflect daily operational realities in every organization working with modern APIs. In the chapters that follow, you'll learn how to implement design patterns that address these use cases directly — with real architectures, platform-specific guidance, and production-grade practices.

Chapter 2: The Evolution of API Gateway Design Patterns

2.1 The Shift from Monoliths to Microservices

Before we can understand the evolution of API gateway design patterns, we need to revisit how application architecture has evolved over the past two decades. This isn't just a history lesson — it's foundational to understanding why gateways were born and how they've adapted alongside the systems they serve.

The Monolithic Era

In traditional enterprise systems, applications were built as monoliths. The entire codebase — from user interface to business logic to database access — was bundled together and deployed as a single unit. Communication between modules was internal, typically within the same runtime environment. There were no REST endpoints to manage, no external clients making granular API calls, and certainly no distributed service networks to coordinate.

Back then, if you needed to expose data to a third party or front-end application, you'd create a web service or some external integration layer — often built as an afterthought.

The Emergence of APIs

As organizations began to embrace web-based platforms, mobile apps, and third-party integrations, APIs emerged as the bridge between internal systems and external consumers. But with APIs came new challenges: authentication, throttling, protocol translation, and observability.

This led to early attempts at API management, often using reverse proxies or custom middleware. These worked, but only up to a point. As systems scaled and customer demands grew, these solutions became brittle, hard to maintain, and deeply coupled to business logic.

Breaking the Monolith: Enter Microservices

The shift to microservices changed everything. Instead of building one large system, applications were now designed as collections of small, independently deployed services — each with its own logic, runtime, and API.

With microservices came a surge in API traffic. Internal services were now calling each other over HTTP or gRPC, and external clients had to deal with fragmented, inconsistent interfaces. API management was no longer optional — it became essential to system stability and developer sanity.

The API gateway became a solution to a new class of problems:

- Unifying fragmented service APIs

- Managing explosive inter-service communication

- Securing and routing traffic with consistency

This transformation created the foundation for the modern API gateway as we know it today.

2.2 From NGINX to Kong: Evolution of Gateways

As the need for smarter traffic control grew, so did the tools. The API gateway didn't appear out of thin air — it evolved from existing web server and proxy technologies, adapting to new architectural demands.

The Role of NGINX and Apache

Tools like NGINX and Apache HTTP Server were initially built as web servers and reverse proxies. They handled SSL termination, basic routing, and some caching — perfect for serving traditional web apps. Over time, developers began repurposing these tools to handle API traffic as well.

With plugins and modules, NGINX could authenticate users, rewrite URLs, apply load balancing strategies, and even integrate with caching systems like Varnish. These were the building blocks of early gateway-like behavior — but they lacked first-class API management features.

The Rise of API-Centric Gateways

As API consumption exploded — thanks to mobile apps, B2B integrations, and cloud services — it became clear that something more specialized was needed. That's where dedicated API gateways entered the picture.

Key Milestones:

- Kong (2015): One of the first open-source gateways built specifically for APIs, leveraging NGINX under the hood and providing a plugin-based architecture for extending functionality.

- Tyk and KrakenD: Other open-source options that emphasized simplicity, scalability, and centralized management.

- AWS API Gateway, Azure API Management, GCP Apigee: Cloud-native offerings that tightly integrated with each provider's ecosystem — reducing the need for infrastructure management.

- Envoy Proxy (2016): Originally created by Lyft, Envoy brought modern service proxy features with observability, extensibility, and native support for HTTP/2 and gRPC. It would later become the foundation of service meshes like Istio.

What Differentiated These Gateways?

The major evolution wasn't just in performance or routing features — it was in how they approached the API lifecycle:

- Developer experience: Built-in portals, docs, API key issuance.

- Policy enforcement: Authentication, quota management, and role-based access.

- Analytics: Request logging, latency dashboards, error reporting.

- Plugin systems: Lua scripts (Kong), middleware (Express Gateway), or cloud policies.

The transition from NGINX-as-a-reverse-proxy to Kong-as-an-API-gateway signaled a broader shift: from infrastructure-focused tools to API-first platforms designed to handle scale, security, and automation.

2.3 Service Mesh vs API Gateway

One of the most common sources of confusion in modern architectures is the overlap between service meshes and API gateways. While they can seem similar — and both often involve traffic control, policies, and observability — they solve fundamentally different problems and operate at different layers of the stack.

What is a Service Mesh?

A service mesh is an infrastructure layer that manages internal service-to-service communication in a microservices environment. It's typically composed of:

- A data plane: Sidecar proxies (like Envoy) deployed alongside every service.

- A control plane: A centralized brain (e.g., Istio, Linkerd, Consul Connect) that manages configuration, policies, and telemetry.

Service meshes handle:

- Automatic retries and circuit breakers

- mTLS for internal communication

- Service discovery

- Traffic shaping and fault injection

- Telemetry collection

They work inside the system, enabling zero-trust communication among services and simplifying resilience features without rewriting business logic.

What Does the API Gateway Handle?

In contrast, an API gateway manages external-to-internal traffic — typically from:

- Web and mobile clients

- Third-party partners

- External services

The gateway is the north-south traffic controller, while the service mesh handles east-west communication.

Feature	API Gateway	Service Mesh
External Client Access	☑	✖
Internal Service Communication	✖	☑
Token Validation / OAuth	☑	⚠ (limited)
TLS for Internal APIs	✖	☑
Observability	☑	☑
Developer Portal	☑	✖
Plugin Ecosystem / Custom Logic	☑	⚠ (limited via filters)

Can They Coexist?

Absolutely. In fact, in many complex cloud environments, they must coexist.

Typical architecture:

- API Gateway: Authenticates client requests, applies rate limits, and routes to internal services.

- Service Mesh: Ensures that once the request is inside the network, it's handled securely, reliably, and observably between services.

The key is knowing where their responsibilities end — and avoiding overlap that creates unnecessary complexity.

2.4 Serverless, Containers, and Edge Considerations

As application deployment models have diversified, API gateways have had to adapt. The emergence of serverless functions, container orchestration, and edge computing has expanded the expectations placed on gateway design.

Serverless: Stateless and Ephemeral

Serverless platforms (AWS Lambda, Azure Functions, Google Cloud Functions) allow developers to deploy small, single-purpose functions without managing infrastructure. These functions are often triggered by HTTP calls, which makes API gateways indispensable.

In a serverless world:

- The gateway authenticates the request

- It validates payloads or headers

- It routes traffic to the correct function

- It may transform the request into a format the function expects

Without an API gateway, serverless architectures would be highly fragmented and insecure.

Example:

A public signup endpoint backed by AWS Lambda might need:

- JWT validation

- Rate limiting (to avoid spam)

- CORS headers

- Path-based routing (e.g., /signup, /login, /reset-password)

All of these are handled at the gateway layer before the request even reaches Lambda.

Containers and Kubernetes

When using containers and Kubernetes, gateways play a similar role, but there's an added layer of orchestration.

- Gateways often work with Ingress controllers to handle routing at the cluster edge.

- In Kubernetes-native systems, NGINX Ingress, Traefik, and Istio Gateway are common tools.

- Gateways must integrate with service discovery and adapt to dynamic scaling — services can appear, disappear, or be rescheduled at any time.

This demands more than just static routing. API gateways must be infrastructure-aware, responding to changes in the cluster without manual intervention.

Edge Computing

Edge computing introduces yet another consideration: moving compute and logic closer to the user — at the CDN layer or on specialized edge nodes.

API gateways must now:

- Serve content and route traffic based on geolocation

- Cache API responses or act as a thin layer before invoking cloud resources

- Apply security policies before requests ever reach core infrastructure

Cloudflare Workers, AWS CloudFront with Lambda@Edge, and Akamai EdgeWorkers are examples of edge-based environments that benefit from gateway logic running at the edge.

These new deployment models have expanded what we expect from gateways — they're no longer just middlemen; they're platform-level components that enforce business logic, security, and reliability at scale.

2.5 Future Trends in API Gateway Architecture

The story of API gateways is far from over. As cloud infrastructure matures and application demands increase, gateways are evolving in several notable directions.

1. Event-Driven Gateways

Most gateways today are HTTP-focused, but event-driven architecture is on the rise. In the future:

- Gateways may need to handle event ingestion, transformation, and routing — not just REST or gRPC.

- Integration with message brokers like Kafka or NATS may become first-class features.

2. AI-Powered Gateways

Machine learning is finding its way into infrastructure:

- Predictive routing (based on traffic patterns)

- Anomaly detection (identifying abusive patterns)

- Dynamic policy adjustment (e.g., throttling based on ML models)

AI-enhanced gateways could offer adaptive protection and traffic management far beyond static configurations.

3. Decentralized and Federated API Control

As more companies operate across clouds, regions, and subsidiaries, managing APIs centrally becomes harder.

- Expect to see more federated API gateways, where local control is maintained but global policies are still enforced.

- Think multi-tenant, multi-region gateways that synchronize with a global control plane.

4. Deep Developer Tooling

Gateways will become more developer-friendly, with:

- CLI tools and SDKs for rapid configuration

- Integration with popular API definition formats (OpenAPI, AsyncAPI)

- Visual interfaces for policy chaining and testing

5. Service Mesh Integration Will Normalize

Rather than being seen as competing technologies, gateway-mesh interoperability will become the standard. Expect seamless traffic routing from external clients through a gateway and into a mesh — all with unified telemetry and policy control.

6. Zero Trust by Default

With security threats escalating, Zero Trust models will become baseline:

- Every API call must be authenticated and authorized.

- Mutual TLS will be enforced.

- Trust will be contextual — evaluated on every request, every time.

Gateways will no longer just support these practices — they'll enforce them by design.

As application architecture continues to evolve, the role of the API gateway grows in both scope and importance. From simple routing tools to full-blown platforms for managing APIs, traffic, and trust — gateways have become foundational to building scalable, secure, and observable systems in the cloud.

The chapters ahead will equip you with the patterns, examples, and vendor-specific implementations to bring this architecture to life in your own environment.

Chapter 3: Core Components and Deployment Models

As cloud-native systems become more complex, the way we deploy, organize, and operate API gateways becomes just as critical as the patterns they enforce. The gateway is no longer a monolithic piece of infrastructure. It is a composable, policy-enforcing, traffic-directing control layer that can take many forms — internal or external, centralized or decentralized, on-prem or in the cloud.

Understanding the core components of a gateway, as well as the architectural models in which it operates, is essential for making informed design decisions. These choices impact latency, security, reliability, and scalability across your system.

3.1 Internal vs External Gateways

Not all gateways are created equal — nor are they all meant to face the same types of traffic. A key architectural distinction lies in whether a gateway is external-facing (also known as an edge gateway) or internal-facing (an intra-cluster or service-level gateway).

External Gateways (Edge Gateways)

These are placed at the boundary of your system, acting as the first point of contact for external clients. Their primary responsibilities include:

- Authentication and authorization

- TLS termination

- Rate limiting and usage quotas

- CORS enforcement

- Path-based routing to internal services

They are optimized for north-south traffic — traffic entering and exiting your network. These gateways must be resilient to attacks, handle high-throughput loads, and provide clear observability.

Examples:

- AWS API Gateway

- Azure API Management Gateway

- NGINX at the edge

- Kong Gateway deployed before Kubernetes ingress

Typical Use Cases:

- Mobile apps hitting /api/v1/

- Partner integrations requiring API keys

- Exposing public GraphQL endpoints

Internal Gateways

Internal gateways sit within the boundary of your network, handling east-west traffic — that is, communication between internal services.

Their primary functions are:

- Routing between services based on domain or request metadata

- Service discovery

- Policy enforcement for internal traffic

- mTLS and service-to-service authentication

- Observability and tracing

These gateways are often part of a service mesh or deployed as lightweight proxies closer to the services themselves.

Examples:

- Istio ingress gateway

- Linkerd with internal policies

- Envoy-based internal proxies

- NGINX running inside the cluster

When to Use Both:

In real-world systems, especially those operating at scale or across environments, both types of gateways are used together:

- External gateway filters and validates requests from the outside.

- Internal gateway ensures secure, observable routing between backend services.

Understanding where to place these components — and how to separate their concerns — is the first step to building robust gateway architectures.

3.2 Ingress Controllers in Kubernetes

In Kubernetes-based environments, managing external access to services is done primarily through Ingress resources. While Kubernetes offers a native Ingress API, it doesn't implement the logic itself — this is delegated to something called an Ingress Controller.

What is an Ingress Controller?

An Ingress Controller is a gateway implementation that watches Kubernetes Ingress resources and translates them into actual routing rules for the underlying proxy or server.

Common Ingress Controllers:

- NGINX Ingress Controller (by far the most used)

- Kong Ingress Controller (combines with Kong Gateway)

- Traefik (lightweight and dynamic)

- HAProxy Ingress

- Istio Gateway (via Envoy)

Why Kubernetes Needs This Abstraction

Kubernetes itself does not handle:

- SSL termination

- Authentication

- Rate limiting

- Traffic splitting

- Path rewrites

The Ingress Controller brings this functionality by plugging into existing proxy software. It listens to Ingress and Service resources and applies changes in near real-time.

Key Capabilities of an Ingress Controller:

- Dynamic configuration reloading based on changes to Ingress manifests

- Integration with cert-manager for automatic TLS certificate management

- Support for canary releases using annotations or custom CRDs

- Authentication plugins (e.g., JWT, OAuth2)

- Metrics and logging via Prometheus, Fluentd, etc.

Limitations of the Default Ingress

The native Kubernetes Ingress resource is relatively limited. Advanced features like rate limiting, custom headers, or advanced routing typically require:

- Annotations (often controller-specific)

- Custom Resource Definitions (CRDs) — such as KongIngress, VirtualService (Istio), or Middleware (Traefik)

In complex Kubernetes environments, it's common to combine an ingress controller with a broader API gateway solution. For example:

- Use Kong Ingress Controller for API management + Kubernetes-native routing.

- Use Istio Gateway as ingress for service mesh-based policies.

This hybrid approach enables both developer simplicity (via YAML manifests) and enterprise features like API key management, quota enforcement, and observability.

3.3 Centralized vs Decentralized Gateways

Another critical deployment consideration is whether your API gateway architecture is centralized or decentralized. Each model has distinct advantages and trade-offs, and the right choice depends on your organizational structure, team autonomy, scalability requirements, and security posture.

Centralized Gateway Model

In a centralized model:

- A single gateway or gateway cluster handles all incoming traffic.

- Policies are managed centrally, typically by a platform or DevOps team.

- All services are registered and managed through the same gateway interface.

Benefits:

- Easier to enforce consistent security and logging policies

- Single point for analytics and debugging

- Unified developer onboarding (e.g., one developer portal)

Challenges:

- Can become a bottleneck as traffic or services scale

- Changes require coordination across teams

- More difficult to support multi-region or multi-team autonomy

Decentralized Gateway Model

In this model, each team, application, or domain can run its own API gateway instance or configuration.

Benefits:

- Teams operate independently and deploy faster

- Ideal for multi-tenant or multi-region setups

- Easier to customize policies per environment

Challenges:

- Harder to maintain policy consistency

- Observability may be fragmented across gateways

- Increased operational complexity

Some organizations adopt a federated approach — centralized governance (e.g., base policies, shared services), combined with team-level autonomy for configurations, plugins, and routing rules.

This balance allows scale without losing visibility or security control — a key pattern in large enterprise and multi-cloud systems.

3.4 API Gateway as a Service (GaaS)

Managing infrastructure for gateways — provisioning servers, updating plugins, scaling clusters — can become a full-time job. To simplify this, many organizations turn to API Gateway as a Service (GaaS) platforms.

These are fully managed offerings provided by cloud vendors or third-party companies that handle the heavy lifting for you.

Leading GaaS Options:

- AWS API Gateway: Native support for Lambda, EC2, and container backends; automatic scaling; usage plans; WAF integration.

- Azure API Management: Developer portal, versioning, policy engine; integrates with Logic Apps and Azure Functions.

- Google Apigee: Enterprise-grade gateway with monetization, analytics, and hybrid deployments.

- Kong Konnect Cloud: SaaS platform for managing Kong Gateways with runtime decoupling.

Core Benefits:

- No infrastructure management — provisioning, patching, and scaling are handled by the provider.

- Out-of-the-box integrations with authentication providers, monitoring tools, and CDNs.

- Instant access to dashboards for analytics, policy enforcement, and usage reports.

- Security and compliance features (e.g., ISO, SOC 2) built-in.

Limitations to Consider:

- Cost models can be unpredictable under high load.

- Vendor lock-in concerns if APIs or policies are not portable.

- May lack fine-grained control over routing behavior or plugin logic.

- Some offerings have cold start issues or rate limit ceilings.

GaaS is a great choice for teams that want to move fast, stay secure, and avoid infrastructure overhead — especially in greenfield projects or API-driven startups. For complex enterprise needs, hybrid GaaS + on-prem models can also work effectively.

3.5 Deployment Scenarios: On-Prem, Cloud, and Hybrid

Where and how you deploy your API gateway is a fundamental architectural decision. Your deployment model affects latency, security, compliance, and integration with existing systems.

Let's walk through the most common deployment scenarios.

1. On-Premise Deployment

This involves installing the gateway software within your own data center or private cloud environment.

Use Cases:

- Highly regulated industries (finance, healthcare, government)

- Systems with no public internet access

- Need to integrate with legacy, on-prem services

Pros:

- Full control over environment, security, and performance

- No external dependencies

- Easier compliance for data residency laws

Cons:

- Requires in-house infrastructure and expertise

- Slower to scale and update

- May lack modern integrations or analytics tools

Examples:

- Kong OSS or Enterprise on VM clusters

- NGINX reverse proxy clusters

- Apigee Hybrid Mode

---

2. Fully Cloud-Hosted

Gateways are deployed in public cloud environments — often using managed services.

Use Cases:

- Cloud-native startups and digital platforms

- Teams focused on speed and agility

- APIs exposed to public or global clients

Pros:

- Automatic scaling and resilience

- Easy integration with cloud-native services

- Built-in monitoring and security tools

Cons:

- Potential latency to on-prem systems

- May require compliance sign-offs

- Cost management can be challenging at scale

Examples:

- AWS API Gateway with Lambda

- Azure API Management with Logic Apps

- Kong Gateway on Kubernetes via EKS/GKE/AKS

---

3. Hybrid Deployment

Combining on-premise and cloud gateways is common in large organizations undergoing digital transformation.

Use Cases:

- Gradual migration from legacy systems to cloud

- Organizations with sensitive data stored on-prem

- Distributed teams with local compliance needs

Pros:

- Flexibility to optimize for performance and compliance

- Leverage cloud innovation while maintaining control

- Enables data and compute proximity

Cons:

- Requires careful coordination between gateway instances

- Configuration management and policy sync can get complex

- Observability and security posture must span both domains

Architecture Tip:

Use a central control plane (e.g., Apigee, Kong Konnect, Tyk Dashboard) with regional or on-prem runtimes to balance control with flexibility.

Final Thoughts on Deployment Models

There's no one-size-fits-all approach when it comes to gateway deployment. The best strategy depends on:

- Your team structure and autonomy needs

- Your compliance and data sovereignty requirements

- The volume and nature of your API traffic

- Your appetite for infrastructure ownership

Some of the most resilient architectures today combine:

- Cloud-native GaaS for public API exposure

- Internal gateways for microservices routing

- Ingress controllers for Kubernetes-native services

- Edge proxies for ultra-low-latency responses

Understanding these components — and deploying them in harmony — is what separates fragile systems from those that scale reliably across environments and across time.

PART II — Design Patterns That Power Scalable Cloud Systems

With the foundational concepts and deployment models in place, Part II shifts the focus to the core design patterns that enable API gateways to scale, secure, and simplify cloud-native systems. These patterns are not theoretical; they represent proven architectural solutions used by leading technology companies, cloud platforms, and DevOps teams in production environments.

Each chapter in this part presents a specific gateway pattern — such as the Edge Gateway, Backend-for-Frontend (BFF), Aggregator, or Gateway Offloading — and breaks it down into practical, actionable components. You'll learn the purpose of the pattern, the problems it solves, how to implement it across various platforms, and the trade-offs involved in real-world scenarios.

Whether you're optimizing for performance, modularity, or developer experience, these patterns form the architectural toolkit for designing resilient and flexible API infrastructures in the cloud. Use them as blueprints to guide your own gateway strategy, no matter what stage of growth or complexity your system is in.

Chapter 4: Edge Gateway Pattern

4.1 Design Overview

At the outermost boundary of any cloud-based architecture lies a critical layer — the Edge Gateway. It is the first component in your infrastructure stack that receives client traffic and, therefore, the first opportunity to enforce security, inspect requests, apply rate limits, and route traffic to internal services.

The Edge Gateway Pattern is a foundational design model where an API gateway is deployed at the "edge" of a system — typically just behind a DNS layer, CDN, or external load balancer. It is purpose-built for north-south traffic (i.e., traffic coming in from external users or systems into your platform).

This pattern is about much more than just routing. An edge gateway sits between a fast-moving, public internet and the controlled environment of your microservices or internal APIs. It must:

- Protect your system from malicious requests, spikes in usage, or unauthorized access.

- Standardize incoming requests and responses, regardless of where they originate.

- Offload expensive tasks like TLS encryption or protocol translation from internal services.

- Shape traffic based on routes, headers, geo-locations, or client credentials.

The Edge Gateway Pattern forms the first line of defense, the first policy enforcement point, and often the first observability hook into your cloud system. It enables internal services to stay lean and focused, while the edge handles client complexity, security hardening, and performance optimization.

4.2 Handling North-South Traffic

The distinction between north-south and east-west traffic is fundamental in distributed systems. North-south refers to the ingress and egress traffic — that is, communication between the external world and your internal services. East-west refers to internal service-to-service traffic within your system or cluster.

The edge gateway is specifically optimized to manage north-south flows. Here's what that involves:

1. Public Client Traffic Control

Mobile apps, browsers, partner systems, IoT devices — all external clients must hit a single point of entry. The edge gateway filters and routes these requests:

- Applies authentication (e.g., JWT, API keys, OAuth2)

- Enforces rate limits and quotas per user or endpoint

- Routes requests to the correct internal service or API version

- Rejects invalid or malformed requests early, before they hit internal systems

2. Simplification of Internal APIs

Backend services no longer need to expose themselves directly to the internet. They remain behind private networks, shielded from DDoS attempts or scanning bots. The edge gateway handles:

- Request transformation (e.g., mapping public-friendly URLs to internal APIs)

- Header injection or cleanup

- Centralized access logging and auditing

3. Support for Multi-Tenant or Multi-Product APIs

A well-configured edge gateway can separate traffic across multiple environments or clients, even if they share the same domain. For example:

- /api/customer-a/* routes to a different backend than /api/customer-b/*

- Query parameters or headers may indicate routing logic

- Dynamic policies based on tokens or API plans

4. Observability and Telemetry at the Edge

Since all traffic flows through the edge gateway, it's the best place to collect:

- Latency metrics

- Request/response logs

- Geolocation data

- Error codes and patterns

This data feeds into monitoring systems like Prometheus, Datadog, or custom dashboards — making the edge a valuable point for analytics and alerting.

The Edge Gateway Pattern enables a clean contract between your external consumers and your internal systems — a buffer that improves maintainability, resilience, and visibility.

4.3 TLS Termination and Forwarding

TLS termination is one of the most resource-intensive but critical functions of an edge gateway. Clients expect HTTPS encryption for every interaction — whether they're submitting login credentials, uploading documents, or calling a RESTful API.

If every internal service handled its own TLS termination, the result would be:

- Inconsistent configuration across services

- Increased CPU usage for encryption/decryption

- Duplication of certificate renewal logic

- Vulnerability to misconfigurations and expired certs

Benefits of Terminating TLS at the Edge

1. Centralized certificate management: Use Let's Encrypt, AWS ACM, or custom certs at the edge without distributing secrets across services.

2. Better performance: Internal traffic can remain unencrypted (or encrypted at lower overhead), improving efficiency.

3. Standardized encryption policies: Enforce TLS 1.2+, set HSTS headers, and block insecure ciphers across all traffic.

4. Simplified client configuration: All clients connect via a single public endpoint (e.g., https://api.example.com).

TLS Forwarding and Re-Encryption

In regulated industries, even internal traffic may need to remain encrypted. In these cases:

- The edge gateway terminates TLS for inspection/logging.

- It then re-encrypts the request using a separate internal certificate before forwarding to downstream services.

This "TLS passthrough" or TLS bridging configuration enables security auditing and traffic inspection without violating end-to-end encryption requirements.

Key Design Considerations

- Use SNI (Server Name Indication) for multi-domain TLS termination.

- Automate certificate renewal via ACME protocol where possible.

- Monitor certificate expiry, cipher usage, and handshake errors.

- For Kubernetes users, use cert-manager with ingress controllers for automated TLS lifecycle management.

In the edge gateway pattern, handling TLS termination efficiently, securely, and centrally is non-negotiable.

4.4 Integration with CDN and WAF

An edge gateway doesn't exist in isolation. It's often part of a stacked perimeter architecture, where performance and security layers are combined. Two critical integrations in this pattern are Content Delivery Networks (CDNs) and Web Application Firewalls (WAFs).

CDN Integration

CDNs (e.g., Cloudflare, Akamai, Fastly, AWS CloudFront) accelerate global delivery by caching responses closer to the user. When integrated properly:

- Static assets (images, scripts, large payloads) are served from edge locations.

- API responses can also be cached — e.g., public product listings, metadata.

Edge gateway + CDN considerations:

- Gateways must respect Cache-Control headers.

- Route cacheable paths to CDN; route dynamic or personalized paths to origin.

- CDNs can reduce traffic hitting your gateway by up to 80%, lowering cost and improving latency.

Some CDNs (like Cloudflare Workers or Fastly Compute@Edge) can even execute lightweight code at the edge — enabling basic routing, request shaping, or validation before the gateway is hit.

WAF Integration

A Web Application Firewall adds an extra security layer before traffic reaches your gateway or backend services.

WAFs:

- Detect and block malicious payloads, SQL injection attempts, cross-site scripting, etc.

- Apply rules based on OWASP Top 10 threats.

- Monitor for anomalies and block bot traffic.

When integrated before or at the edge gateway:

- All client traffic is inspected before it hits internal logic.

- Threats are neutralized early.

- Security teams can monitor WAF dashboards and alerts in real time.

WAF placement strategies:

- Some gateways (e.g., AWS API Gateway with AWS WAF) support native integration.

- Others integrate with external appliances or cloud-based WAFs via routing or DNS settings.

- In Kubernetes, you might use tools like ModSecurity (via NGINX) or integrate with providers like Cloud Armor (GCP) or Azure Front Door.

Together, CDN and WAF transform a basic gateway into a fully fortified and globally performant edge layer — capable of handling scale, security, and low-latency delivery with confidence.

4.5 Example: NGINX as Edge Gateway

To bring the Edge Gateway Pattern to life, let's walk through a practical example using NGINX — one of the most battle-tested and widely used tools for edge traffic management.

Use Case Scenario:

You're operating a multi-service SaaS platform with:

- A public API served at api.example.com

- Services running behind a Kubernetes cluster

- A need to terminate TLS, apply rate limits, and route traffic to appropriate backends

NGINX Configuration Example:

nginx

CopyEdit

```
http {
    log_format main '$remote_addr - $remote_user [$time_local] "$request" '
                    '$status $body_bytes_sent "$http_referer" '
                    '"$http_user_agent" "$http_x_forwarded_for"';

    access_log /var/log/nginx/access.log main;

    limit_req_zone $binary_remote_addr zone=api_limit:10m rate=10r/s;

    server {
```

```
listen 443 ssl;

server_name api.example.com;


ssl_certificate /etc/ssl/certs/api.crt;

ssl_certificate_key /etc/ssl/private/api.key;


location /v1/ {

    limit_req zone=api_limit burst=20;

    proxy_pass http://backend_v1;

    proxy_set_header Host $host;

    proxy_set_header X-Real-IP $remote_addr;

}


location /v2/ {

    proxy_pass http://backend_v2;

    proxy_set_header Host $host;

    proxy_set_header X-Forwarded-For $proxy_add_x_forwarded_for;

}

}
```

Features Implemented:

- TLS termination with provided SSL certs

- Rate limiting at 10 requests/second per IP

- Header injection for forwarding real IPs and host info

- Routing based on API version path (/v1/, /v2/)

Extending the Gateway:

- Add auth_request directives for external OAuth2 validation

- Integrate with Lua modules or OpenResty for token validation

- Use caching modules to store responses for GET endpoints

- Configure logging to push into ELK stack or CloudWatch

Deployment Context:

- Deployed as a Docker container on edge nodes

- Managed via Ansible or Helm charts

- Paired with Cloudflare CDN for asset caching and DDoS protection

This setup provides a production-grade edge gateway with minimal overhead, high flexibility, and broad ecosystem support — a great starting point for teams building scalable and secure APIs.

Closing Thoughts on the Edge Gateway Pattern

The edge is more than a technical perimeter — it's where performance, security, and scalability collide. The Edge Gateway Pattern is one of the most important in the modern API architecture toolkit. Whether implemented using NGINX, Kong, or a managed service, the principles remain the same: protect, route, observe, and offload.

A well-architected edge layer buys you safety, speed, and control — all prerequisites for a resilient, cloud-native platform.

Chapter 5: Backend-for-Frontend (BFF) Pattern

5.1 Why BFF is Needed

Modern applications serve a variety of clients — mobile apps, web apps, smart TVs, voice assistants, and IoT devices — each with different expectations, bandwidth, rendering capabilities, and interaction models. Yet the traditional model of a single, one-size-fits-all API often fails to meet these varied needs efficiently.

The Backend-for-Frontend (BFF) pattern emerged to solve this disconnect. It is a design model where each type of client has its own tailored backend gateway, often referred to as a "BFF," which sits between the client and the underlying services.

This pattern recognizes that one API does not fit all:

- Mobile clients need lighter payloads due to network constraints.

- Web apps may require multiple aggregated calls to render a single view.

- IoT devices demand low latency, with simplified authentication and consistent heartbeat endpoints.

By introducing client-specific gateways, BFFs bridge the gap between frontend demands and backend service realities. They help optimize request structures, hide internal complexity, and align backend data with UI consumption models.

More importantly, they enable frontend teams to iterate independently by owning their own backend layer — without impacting core service logic or API stability for other clients.

The BFF pattern doesn't replace the edge gateway or internal gateways — it complements them. In a layered architecture:

- The edge gateway handles north-south traffic, security, and global routing.

- The BFF handles view orchestration and UI-centric data shaping.

- The internal services handle domain logic and persistence.

5.2 Per-Client Gateways (Web, Mobile, IoT)

A key principle of the BFF pattern is differentiating clients and building APIs that serve their unique requirements. This means constructing separate backend layers for each type of frontend — whether web, mobile, or device-based.

1. Web BFF

A BFF for web applications may support:

- Server-side rendered content (SSR)

- Real-time socket connections

- Session-based auth (cookies, CSRF tokens)

- Pagination, sorting, and UI-specific filters

- Integration with analytics or tracking

Design example:

- Web app sends a single request to /dashboard

- Web BFF calls UserService, ActivityService, and SettingsService

- Combines and returns a normalized response for rendering the page

2. Mobile BFF

Mobile apps have different concerns:

- Limited bandwidth, higher latency

- Token-based authentication (OAuth2, JWT)

- Battery and memory constraints

The mobile BFF:

- Compresses payloads

- Reduces API round-trips by aggregating data

- Applies mobile-specific logic (e.g., offline queuing)

Design example:

- Mobile app requests /home-screen

- BFF responds with just the top-level essentials (e.g., alerts, metrics)

- Actual details are lazily loaded by client logic

3. IoT / Device BFF

IoT devices are minimalistic:

- Use MQTT, CoAP, or lightweight HTTP

- Require long-lived connections or periodic polling

- Need idempotent commands and simplified auth

A BFF here translates HTTP/gRPC to device protocols or vice versa, and may act as:

- Protocol adapter

- Throttler

- Heartbeat and command-response manager

Design example:

- Device sends a ping or telemetry every 10s

- BFF stores and routes this to TelemetryService while enforcing rate limits

Summary Comparison Table:

Feature	Web BFF	Mobile BFF	IoT BFF
Auth Mechanism	Cookie/session	OAuth2/JWT	Pre-shared key
Payload Optimization	Medium	High	Very High
UI Aggregation	Yes	Yes	No
Protocol Support	HTTP/WebSocket	HTTP	MQTT/CoAP
Usage Pattern	Complex views	Frequent syncs	Periodic polling

The BFF pattern lets teams fine-tune backend logic based on what the frontend actually needs — leading to faster apps, better UX, and clearer ownership boundaries.

5.3 GraphQL and REST in BFF

One of the core advantages of the BFF pattern is that it gives teams flexibility to choose the best API style for each client — and this often leads to the question: REST or GraphQL?

REST in BFF

Traditional REST APIs still work very well within the BFF model:

- Clearly defined endpoints

- Mature support in most tools and frameworks

- Great fit for predictable, coarse-grained data (e.g., GET /orders)

REST can be used in BFFs to aggregate several internal service calls behind a single endpoint.

Example:

http

CopyEdit

GET /bff/dashboard

This could call:

- /user/profile

- /account/balance

- /notifications?limit=3

And return a flattened, frontend-friendly response — without the frontend having to juggle 3 separate requests.

GraphQL in BFF

GraphQL is especially compelling for BFFs because:

- The frontend controls exactly what data it receives

- The schema is strongly typed and introspectable

- It reduces the need for multiple round-trips

GraphQL works well when:

- The client UI changes frequently

- The data model is complex or nested

- You want to reduce over-fetching and under-fetching

In this setup:

- The BFF exposes a GraphQL endpoint

- It acts as an orchestrator — mapping GraphQL queries to backend REST or gRPC calls

- It may implement resolvers that fetch from services like ProductService, CartService, etc.

Hybrid Use Case:
A mobile BFF might expose:

- REST for critical paths (POST /checkout)

- GraphQL for dynamic content (/graphql endpoint used by product listing views)

The decision between GraphQL and REST doesn't have to be binary. In BFFs, they can coexist and complement each other — with REST used for command paths, and GraphQL for rich data fetching.

5.4 Practical Scenarios and Sample Architectures

Let's examine real-world scenarios where the BFF pattern provides structure, optimization, and autonomy.

Scenario 1: E-commerce Platform with Multi-Client Support

Problem:
Frontend teams struggle to consume the same REST API. Web UI requires detailed product metadata, mobile just needs titles and prices, and the marketing team wants to track click-through events.

BFF Solution:

- Web BFF: fetches deep product metadata, supports preview and edit flows

- Mobile BFF: serves condensed product cards, applies mobile rate limits

- Marketing BFF: handles analytics ingestion and short-lived campaign endpoints

Benefits:

- Clients operate independently

- Backend services are protected from client-specific quirks

- Teams ship faster without breaking each other's workflows

Scenario 2: Multi-Tenant SaaS Platform

Problem:
Each customer (tenant) has custom business rules and UI configurations. Core services are shared, but presentation logic varies widely.

BFF Solution:
Each tenant gets a tenant-specific BFF:

- Enforces branding and feature flags

- Transforms backend data formats

- Handles tenant-scoped rate limits and tokens

Benefits:

- Core services stay generic

- BFFs enforce tenant isolation

- Custom logic lives at the gateway edge, not in core APIs

Sample Architecture Diagram:

plaintext

CopyEdit

```
            +--------------------+

            |   Edge Gateway     |

            +----------+---------+

                       |

        +--------------+-------------------+

        |              |              |

   +---------+    +------------+   +----------+

   | Web BFF |    | Mobile BFF |   | IoT BFF  |

   +----+----+    +------+------+   +----+------+
```

```
        |            |               |
+----v----+    +------v------+    +------v-----+
| UserSvc |    | ProductSvc |     | Telemetry |
| AuthSvc |    | CartSvc    |     | Commands  |
+---------+    +------------+     +-----------+
```

This separation ensures:

- Security boundaries between client types

- Tailored experiences for each UI

- Easier scaling and debugging

5.5 Example: Express Gateway with BFF

Let's walk through a working example of the BFF pattern using Express Gateway, a Node.js-based open-source API gateway framework designed to be developer-friendly and easily extensible.

Use Case:

A web application dashboard needs to show:

- User profile

- Notifications

- Recent transactions

Rather than making 3 requests from the frontend, we build a BFF to aggregate and return everything in a single call.

Project Setup:

bash

CopyEdit

```
npm install -g express-gateway

eg gateway create bff-dashboard

cd bff-dashboard

npm install axios
```

gateway.config.yml (Simplified):

yaml

CopyEdit

```
http:

  port: 8080
```

```yaml
apiEndpoints:

  dashboard:

    path: /dashboard

    method: GET


serviceEndpoints:

  user:

    url: http://localhost:3001

  notifications:

    url: http://localhost:3002

  transactions:

    url: http://localhost:3003


policies:

  - custom-dashboard-aggregator:

    - action:

        name: bffAggregator


pipelines:
```

dashboard:

  apiEndpoints:

  - dashboard

  policies:

  - custom-dashboard-aggregator: []

Custom Policy (bffAggregator.js):

js

CopyEdit

```js
const axios = require('axios');

module.exports = {
  name: 'bffAggregator',
  policy: () => {
    return async (req, res, next) => {
      try {
        const [user, notifications, transactions] = await Promise.all([
          axios.get('http://localhost:3001/user'),
          axios.get('http://localhost:3002/notifications'),
```

```
    axios.get('http://localhost:3003/transactions')

  ]);


  res.send({

    user: user.data,

    notifications: notifications.data,

    transactions: transactions.data

  });

  } catch (err) {

    res.status(500).send({ error: 'BFF aggregation failed' });

  }

 };

 }

};
```

Result:

- Frontend hits /dashboard

- Gateway aggregates data from 3 internal services

- Response is shaped exactly for UI needs

Benefits:

- Zero duplication of logic in UI

- Backend services remain decoupled

- Gateway handles failover and error masking

Closing Thoughts on the BFF Pattern

The BFF pattern represents a shift from treating gateways as passive proxies to making them smart, client-aware orchestrators. It acknowledges that frontend needs vary widely — and meeting them through a unified API is often unrealistic.

By adopting BFFs:

- You empower frontend teams with autonomy

- You isolate complexity and reduce cross-team dependencies

- You align backend and frontend evolution more cleanly

Chapter 6: Aggregator Pattern

6.1 Pattern Structure

As distributed systems scale, the complexity of interactions between microservices often increases exponentially. What used to be a single endpoint in a monolithic system may now require data from three or more services. In such scenarios, the Aggregator Pattern emerges as a clean solution for simplifying client interactions.

The Aggregator Pattern refers to a design where the API gateway acts as a request orchestrator, aggregating responses from multiple backend services into a single unified response for the client.

At its core, this pattern helps:

- Reduce round-trips between client and server

- Hide backend complexity from external consumers

- Shape responses according to frontend or business needs

- Centralize logic that doesn't belong inside services themselves

The aggregator may live:

- Inside the API gateway itself (via plugins or middleware)

- In a dedicated orchestration layer (such as a Lambda or BFF)

- As part of an internal composite service

Regardless of placement, the goal is the same: collect data from multiple services and return a cohesive response in one call.

Typical Structure:

plaintext

CopyEdit

```
    Client

       |

    /dashboard

       |

    API Gateway

    /  |  \

UserService  OrderService  NotificationService

    \  |  /

    Aggregated JSON Response
```

By consolidating service calls, the aggregator offloads the complexity from clients — particularly mobile apps and SPAs — and improves maintainability across the stack.

6.2 Gateway as API Composer

One of the most valuable capabilities of a modern API gateway is to act as an API composer — merging the results of multiple microservices into a unified contract.

Rather than exposing internal API granularity (e.g., GET /user, GET /orders, GET /notifications), the gateway exposes:

http

CopyEdit

GET /dashboard

And internally:

- Fetches userProfile from UserService

- Fetches recentOrders from OrderService

- Fetches alerts from NotificationService

- Normalizes all the responses

- Returns a single JSON object

This approach is especially valuable when:

- Frontend code should stay simple (no orchestration logic)

- You need to batch multiple service calls efficiently

- There's a need for response shaping to hide backend schemas

Key Advantages:

- Reduced network latency (fewer client-side HTTP calls)

- Improved developer experience for frontend teams

- Flexibility to evolve internal APIs without breaking consumers

Tools and Techniques for Composition:

- Middleware frameworks (Express.js, Fastify) inside BFFs or gateways

- Serverless orchestration functions (e.g., AWS Lambda, Azure Functions)

- Custom plugins in Kong, Envoy, or Express Gateway

- Declarative API composition (e.g., GraphQL resolvers)

In each approach, the gateway doesn't just route — it actively constructs responses that map better to how the UI or partner needs the data.

6.3 Error Handling and Partial Failures

Aggregating multiple services introduces a new class of challenges: what happens when one of the downstream services fails?

Clients still expect consistent behavior, so the aggregator must handle:

- Timeouts

- Network errors

- HTTP 5xx/4xx status codes

- Empty or malformed responses

Common Strategies for Managing Partial Failures:

1. Graceful Degradation

If one service fails, the aggregator still returns a response — possibly with placeholders or fallback values.

json

CopyEdit

```
{
  "user": { "name": "John", "email": "john@example.com" },
  "orders": [],
  "notifications": null,
```

```
"errors": ["Failed to load notifications"]

}
```

Useful for non-critical data like promotional banners or analytics.

2. Client-Driven Degradation

The client includes a header or query parameter to indicate what's optional:

pgsql

CopyEdit

```
GET /dashboard?include=orders,notifications
```

The gateway only fetches the specified resources, reducing error surface.

3. Timeout with Fallback

Set short timeouts for each service. If one exceeds, log the failure and continue.

js

CopyEdit

```
const fetchWithTimeout = (url, timeout) =>
  Promise.race([
    axios.get(url),
    new Promise((_, reject) => setTimeout(() => reject(new Error("Timeout")), timeout))
```

```
]);
```

4. Circuit Breakers

Use libraries like Hystrix, Resilience4j, or Envoy filters to stop calling unstable services temporarily, preventing cascading failures.

5. Structured Error Responses

Return partial successes in a consistent, machine-readable way.

json

CopyEdit

```
{
  "status": "partial_success",
  "data": { ... },
  "errors": [{ "service": "OrderService", "message": "Timeout" }]
}
```

A well-designed aggregator doesn't just glue APIs — it absorbs failure elegantly, maintaining availability and reliability for the client.

6.4 Performance Optimization Techniques

API composition can introduce latency — especially when multiple services must be contacted. Without careful design, response times can spike, and clients may suffer degraded performance.

To mitigate this, gateways can employ several performance-enhancing techniques:

1. Parallel Execution

Call all services asynchronously using parallel promises or threads.

js

CopyEdit

```
const [user, orders, notifications] = await Promise.all([

  getUserData(),

  getRecentOrders(),

  getNotifications()

]);
```

Reduces total response time to that of the slowest call, rather than the sum of all.

2. Response Caching

Cache frequently accessed but slow data — e.g., using Redis, CDN edge caching, or memory cache in Node.js.

- Use short TTLs (e.g., 30s) for fast-changing data

- Cache per-user responses when applicable

- Invalidate on write or state change

3. Field-Level Resolution

Only fetch fields or services if needed. If UI only needs user info, skip calling OrderService.

This technique is often used with GraphQL BFFs.

4. Stale-While-Revalidate

Serve cached data immediately while refreshing it in the background for future requests.

Provides low-latency response with eventual freshness.

5. Payload Optimization

Minimize response size:

- Strip unused fields

- Use Gzip or Brotli compression

- Avoid nested or verbose JSON where not required

6. HTTP/2 Multiplexing

Where supported (e.g., in gRPC, Envoy, or modern browsers), use HTTP/2 to stream requests over a single connection efficiently.

These optimizations ensure that your gateway doesn't become a bottleneck — even while aggregating data from multiple internal systems.

6.5 Example: AWS Lambda + API Gateway Aggregation

Let's walk through a real-world example using AWS Lambda and Amazon API Gateway to implement the Aggregator Pattern.

Use Case:

Expose a /profile endpoint that returns:

- User Info from UserService

- Order History from OrderService

- Recommendations from RecommendationService

Architecture:

plaintext

CopyEdit

Client → API Gateway (/profile) → Lambda Function

↘

Multiple Internal REST Services

Step 1: Define API Gateway Endpoint

In AWS API Gateway (HTTP API or REST API):

- Create GET /profile

- Integrate with a Lambda function

- Enable CORS and caching if needed

Step 2: Lambda Function (Node.js)

js

CopyEdit

```js
const axios = require('axios');

exports.handler = async (event) => {
  try {
    const [user, orders, recommendations] = await Promise.all([
      axios.get('https://internal-api/user'),
      axios.get('https://internal-api/orders'),
      axios.get('https://internal-api/recommendations')
    ]);
```

```
    return {

      statusCode: 200,

      body: JSON.stringify({

        user: user.data,

        orders: orders.data,

        recommendations: recommendations.data

      })

    };


  } catch (err) {

    return {

      statusCode: 206,

      body: JSON.stringify({

        message: "Partial data returned",

        error: err.message

      })

    };

  }
```

Step 3: Deploy and Secure

- Use AWS IAM roles to control which services Lambda can access

- Attach a usage plan or API key to API Gateway if exposing publicly

- Enable CloudWatch Logs for observability

Optional Enhancements:

- Add response caching using API Gateway settings

- Move aggregation logic to Step Functions for more complex workflows

- Use Lambda Powertools (for Node.js or Python) for structured logging and tracing

This example shows how a lightweight Lambda function can act as an effective aggregator — insulating the client from backend fragmentation, while maintaining clarity and flexibility.

Closing Thoughts on the Aggregator Pattern

In complex systems, clients shouldn't have to understand how many services exist, what their schemas look like, or how to combine their outputs. The Aggregator Pattern solves this with elegance — letting your gateway act not just as a router, but as a composer, cache, and shield.

By applying this pattern:

- Frontend developers move faster with simpler APIs

- Backend services remain focused and single-responsibility

- Clients see consistent, performant responses — even in a distributed world

Chapter 7: Gateway Offloading Pattern

7.1 Offloading Authentication

Authentication is one of the most critical but repetitive concerns in distributed systems. Every service that handles incoming requests typically needs to validate identity — but duplicating auth logic across dozens of microservices is not only inefficient, it's risky.

The Gateway Offloading Pattern solves this by delegating common concerns — especially authentication — to the API gateway layer. The gateway, sitting as the first point of contact for incoming traffic, becomes responsible for verifying identity, enforcing security policies, and rejecting unauthorized requests before they ever hit your core services.

Benefits of Offloading Authentication:

- Consistency: All services receive requests from already-authenticated identities.

- Security: Central enforcement of token validation, scopes, and certificate checks.

- Simplification: Internal services trust the gateway and focus only on domain logic.

- Flexibility: Token format or provider can be swapped without changing service code.

Supported Methods:

- JWT validation: Gateway validates JSON Web Tokens and passes claims as headers.

- OAuth2 tokens: Introspects tokens using an authorization server (e.g., Auth0, Keycloak).

- API keys: Manages issuance, quotas, and verification.

- mTLS client certificates: Accepts only pre-authorized client identities at the edge.

- Session cookies: Useful for browser-based clients; validated using encrypted cookies.

Example: Kong JWT Plugin

With Kong Gateway, you can enable JWT auth like this (in declarative YAML):

yaml

CopyEdit

```
plugins:
 - name: jwt
   config:
    claims_to_verify: ["exp"]
    key_claim_name: "iss"
```

secret_is_base64: false

Then each service gets user identity via headers like:

makefile

CopyEdit

x-consumer-id: user_abc123

x-consumer-custom-id: 42

x-consumer-username: jdoe

The gateway takes care of verifying the signature, expiration, and issuer — your microservices receive only verified, trusted requests.

7.2 Caching and Response Transformation

Offloading caching and response transformation is another key element of this pattern. Rather than each service implementing its own logic to cache, compress, or modify responses, the gateway can handle these concerns centrally.

Caching at the Gateway

API gateways can cache entire endpoint responses based on:

- Request path and query parameters

- Authorization headers

- Response headers (e.g., Cache-Control)

This is especially useful for:

- Public GET endpoints (product catalogs, configurations)

- Frequently accessed metadata (e.g., country codes, currencies)

- Data that changes slowly but is requested often

Example: Kong Proxy Caching Plugin

yaml

CopyEdit

```yaml
plugins:
  - name: proxy-cache
    config:
      strategy: memory
      content_type:
        - application/json
      cache_ttl: 300
      request_method:
```

    - GET

This caches eligible responses in memory for 5 minutes, reducing backend load dramatically.

Response Transformation

Sometimes, clients require a different structure than what services provide. Instead of modifying services, the gateway can:

- Add/remove/rename fields

- Format timestamps

- Mask sensitive data (e.g., redact fields)

- Inject headers or CORS responses

Example: Transform Plugin in Kong

yaml

CopyEdit

```
plugins:
  - name: response-transformer
    config:
      remove:
```

json: ["internal_id", "debug_info"]

add:

json: ["gateway_version:1.2.0"]

These transformations happen at the edge, avoiding code duplication and preserving clean service contracts.

7.3 Request Validation and Sanitization

One of the first responsibilities of a well-designed gateway is to ensure only valid requests reach your microservices. This means enforcing schemas, stripping unexpected fields, and rejecting malformed or malicious payloads.

Validation Examples:

- Required headers or query parameters

- Content type checks (Content-Type: application/json)

- Body schema validation (against JSON Schema)

- Enforcing max request body sizes

- Input format checks (e.g., phone numbers, emails)

Sanitization Examples:

- Stripping dangerous inputs (e.g., <script> tags)

- Limiting deeply nested objects

- Removing unused query parameters

- Blocking special characters or SQL injection patterns

By doing this at the gateway:

- Services stay minimal and avoid repeating the same checks

- Malicious or malformed traffic is rejected early

- Logging and audit trails capture violation patterns

Example: Express Gateway Policy for Schema Validation

js

CopyEdit

```js
module.exports = {
  name: 'validate-schema',
  policy: () => (req, res, next) => {
    if (!req.body.email || !req.body.email.includes('@')) {
```

```
    return res.status(400).send({ error: 'Invalid email' });

  }

  next();

  }

};
```

This can be injected into pipelines without modifying downstream services.

JSON Schema-Based Validation

Advanced gateways support defining full schemas via OpenAPI or JSON Schema and automatically rejecting requests that don't comply.

This creates a self-documenting API and guarantees consistency — especially useful for public APIs.

7.4 Integration with Logging and Telemetry Systems

Observability is a fundamental requirement in any distributed system. The API gateway, being the first touchpoint for every request, is a natural place to log, trace, and monitor API usage, latency, and error rates.

Instead of instrumenting every service manually, offloading telemetry to the gateway gives you:

- Centralized logging

- Correlation IDs and request tracing

- Metrics collection per route

- Security auditing

Logs

Gateways can log:

- Request metadata (IP, headers, tokens)

- Response status codes

- Latency (gateway, upstream)

- Auth results and policy violations

These logs can be sent to:

- Cloud-native services (AWS CloudWatch, Azure Monitor)

- Open-source stacks (ELK, Loki, Fluentd)

- SIEMs for security analysis

Tracing

Gateways support distributed tracing using:

- Zipkin

- Jaeger

- OpenTelemetry

- AWS X-Ray

They inject headers like x-request-id, trace-id, and span-id so that backend services can participate in a full request trace.

Metrics

Gateways export Prometheus metrics such as:

- http_requests_total

- http_request_duration_seconds

- gateway_errors_total

- auth_failures_total

These feed into Grafana dashboards or alerting systems for real-time ops visibility.

Example: Kong Prometheus Plugin

yaml

CopyEdit

plugins:

  - name: prometheus

Kong will now expose a /metrics endpoint with real-time gateway metrics, ready to be scraped by Prometheus.

7.5 Example: Kong Gateway Declarative Configs

Let's walk through a practical example where we use Kong Gateway and declarative configuration (YAML) to apply multiple offloading features — authentication, caching, transformation, and logging — with zero code changes in backend services.

Use Case:

Expose a /products endpoint:

- Protected by JWT

- Cached for 5 minutes

- Sensitive fields removed from the response

- Logs forwarded to a syslog server

kong.yaml **Configuration:**

yaml

CopyEdit

```yaml
_format_version: "3.0"

services:

  - name: product-service

    url: http://products.internal:8000


routes:

  - name: products

    paths:

      - /products

    methods:

      - GET

    service: product-service


plugins:

  - name: jwt

    route: products
```

```yaml
    config:
      claims_to_verify: ["exp"]

  - name: proxy-cache
    route: products
    config:
      strategy: memory
      cache_ttl: 300

  - name: response-transformer
    route: products
    config:
      remove:
        json: ["internal_cost", "supply_chain_id"]

  - name: syslog
    route: products
    config:
      host: logs.mycompany.com
```

port: 514

facility: local0

severity: info

Benefits:

- Authentication is enforced before backend is even called.

- Cached responses reduce load for frequent calls.

- Clients never see sensitive fields.

- Logs provide insight into usage and access patterns.

Deployment:

- Load config into Kong via DB-less mode:

bash

CopyEdit

```
KONG_DECLARATIVE_CONFIG=kong.yaml kong start
```

- Or use decK (declarative config CLI) to sync config to a live Kong cluster:

bash

CopyEdit

```
deck sync --config kong.yaml
```

This declarative approach aligns with infrastructure-as-code principles, version control, and CI/CD pipelines — ensuring that your gateway policies are repeatable, auditable, and automated.

Closing Thoughts on the Gateway Offloading Pattern

The Gateway Offloading Pattern is about delegating complexity to where it belongs. API gateways are uniquely positioned to centralize and enforce policies that cut across services — without polluting business logic or creating redundancy.

By offloading:

- Authentication, you reduce attack surfaces and standardize identity checks.

- Caching and transformation, you decouple presentation concerns from data.

- Validation and telemetry, you gain observability and control without burdening developers.

This pattern turns your API gateway into a trustworthy gatekeeper and control plane — a critical component in resilient, secure, and high-performance cloud-native systems.

Chapter 8: Canary and Blue-Green Deployment Pattern

8.1 Progressive Delivery with Gateways

In modern cloud-native development, the ability to release new versions gradually, observe them in production, and react quickly to problems is no longer optional — it's essential.

The Canary and Blue-Green Deployment Pattern is a powerful strategy for progressive delivery, and API gateways serve as a central control point to implement it safely and efficiently.

- Blue-Green Deployment: Maintain two identical environments — blue (current) and green (new). Switch traffic from blue to green instantly or gradually once green is verified.

- Canary Deployment: Deploy the new version (canary) alongside the existing version (stable), and gradually route a percentage of traffic to the canary while monitoring health.

While both strategies aim to minimize risk, canary deployments offer finer control — enabling early detection of issues and selective rollout.

Why Gateways Matter

API gateways operate at the request-routing layer, making them ideal for:

- Controlling traffic flows by percentage or headers

- Routing users based on tokens, geos, or session info

- Rolling back to stable versions instantly

- Measuring real-time metrics before scaling up

Rather than configuring complex service mesh rules or redeploying proxies, the gateway provides a clean, centralized mechanism for progressive delivery.

8.2 Weighted Routing

Weighted routing is at the heart of canary deployments. The gateway directs a configurable percentage of traffic to different backend versions based on routing weights.

How It Works:

- Two backend services (v1 and v2) are registered behind the same endpoint.

- Gateway splits incoming requests based on a percentage:

  - 90% to v1 (stable)

  - 10% to v2 (canary)

- As v2 proves stable, its weight increases (e.g., 25%, 50%, 100%).

- If an error spike is detected, routing is reversed instantly.

Benefits:

- No DNS changes or redeployments

- Safe, controlled exposure to new code

- Real user feedback without full rollout

Use Cases:

- Deploying new business logic (e.g., pricing model)

- Testing new UI APIs with real users

- Verifying new integrations (e.g., payment gateways)

Example: Kong Gateway (Routes with Weights)

yaml

CopyEdit

```
services:
  - name: api-v1
    url: http://api-v1.internal
  - name: api-v2
    url: http://api-v2.internal
```

```
routes:

 - name: canary-route

   paths: ["/api"]

   services:

    - name: api-v1

      weight: 90

    - name: api-v2

      weight: 10
```

Kong distributes traffic using the weights specified. You can script this change or automate it via CI/CD tools.

Example: AWS App Mesh or Istio

Use weighted VirtualService or Route definitions to control upstream percentages dynamically.

8.3 Rollback Mechanisms

No matter how carefully you test, issues in production are inevitable. Gateways help you rollback instantly, without waiting for Kubernetes or server deployments to complete.

Gateway-Level Rollbacks:

- Reduce canary traffic to 0% and restore stable version to 100%

- Can be triggered by metrics (e.g., error rate > 5%) or alerts

- No need to redeploy containers — just adjust routing

How to Implement:

1. Use observability tools (e.g., Datadog, Prometheus) to monitor latency and errors.

2. Define rollback triggers (manual or automated).

3. Integrate rollback logic into your deployment pipeline (e.g., GitHub Actions, Jenkins, Spinnaker).

4. Adjust traffic weights at the gateway using API or CLI.

Example: AWS CloudWatch + Lambda

- Watch for 5xx spikes or p95 latency above thresholds

- Trigger a Lambda to reset traffic weights in AWS App Runner or API Gateway

Kong Deck CLI

bash

CopyEdit

```
deck gateway update --path kong.yaml --traffic-split=v1=100,v2=0
```

This resets routing in seconds — far faster than container redeployments.

Benefits:

- Safe, fast rollback

- No user-visible downtime

- Can be done with or without code changes

A properly configured gateway becomes a safety valve for every release.

8.4 Feature Flags and API Versioning

Progressive delivery doesn't stop at routing traffic. Gateways can also play a role in feature flag management and API versioning, enabling more dynamic rollouts.

Feature Flags at the Gateway

Instead of exposing experimental logic through hard deployments, gateways can:

- Inspect headers, tokens, or cookies

- Route flagged users to alternate backends or enable experimental headers

- Act as the enforcement point for feature rollout

Example:

plaintext

CopyEdit

If `X-Feature-Flag: true` in request → Route to new service

Else → Use default path

This enables gradual exposure to:

- Beta users

- Internal testers

- Specific geographies or device types

You can also integrate with feature flag tools like LaunchDarkly, Unleash, or Flagsmith, letting the gateway read from a centralized store.

API Versioning via Gateway

Gateways simplify the process of maintaining multiple versions of APIs:

- URL-based: /v1/orders vs /v2/orders

- Header-based: Accept-Version: v2

- Hostname-based: v2.api.example.com

The gateway routes requests accordingly, shielding backend services from versioning logic.

Benefits:

- Easier deprecation and sunset of old APIs

- Smooth migration of clients without breaking changes

- Clear control over legacy vs modern traffic

By combining versioning with weighted routing, you can gradually phase out legacy APIs — directing more users to v2 over time and collecting telemetry before turning off v1.

8.5 Example: GCP Cloud Run + Traffic Splitting

Google Cloud Run offers a serverless container platform that integrates directly with traffic splitting — making it an ideal example of the canary and blue-green pattern in action.

Scenario:

You've deployed a new version (v2) of your Cloud Run service and want to:

- Route 10% of traffic to v2

- Monitor logs and error rates

- Gradually ramp up to 100% if stable

Step 1: Deploy v2 Revision

bash

CopyEdit

```
gcloud run deploy my-api \
  --image gcr.io/my-project/my-api:v2 \
  --region us-central1
```

Step 2: Split Traffic Between Revisions

bash

CopyEdit

```
gcloud run services update-traffic my-api \
  --to-revisions "my-api-v1=90,my-api-v2=10"
```

Cloud Run begins routing traffic accordingly without downtime.

Step 3: Observe in Cloud Logging and Metrics

- Use Google Cloud Monitoring to track v2 latency, errors

- If stable, update traffic split:

bash

CopyEdit

```
gcloud run services update-traffic my-api \

  --to-revisions "my-api-v1=50,my-api-v2=50"
```

Eventually:

bash

CopyEdit

```
gcloud run services update-traffic my-api \

  --to-revisions "my-api-v2=100"
```

If a problem arises:

bash

CopyEdit

```
gcloud run services update-traffic my-api \

  --to-revisions "my-api-v1=100"
```

This traffic shift is instant — no container restarts, no DNS changes.

Closing Thoughts on the Canary and Blue-Green Deployment Pattern

Progressive delivery isn't just a deployment strategy — it's a cultural shift toward safer, smarter, more responsive software releases.

With the right API gateway:

- You can route traffic with surgical precision

- Roll back in seconds

- Observe behavior before scaling impact

- Empower teams to iterate with confidence

Whether you're deploying a new backend service, exposing a new version of an API, or testing UI features with real users, the gateway becomes your release control center — reducing risk and improving agility.

Chapter 9: Zero Trust Gateway Security Patterns

9.1 Enforcing Least Privilege Access

The core philosophy behind Zero Trust Architecture (ZTA) is simple but profound: never trust, always verify. In traditional systems, trust was often granted based on location — if a request came from inside the network, it was considered safe. In cloud-native, containerized environments, this trust model is not just outdated — it's dangerous.

Gateways are now front-line enforcers of least privilege access. Instead of trusting the perimeter, the gateway examines every request and enforces fine-grained policies based on identity, context, and compliance.

Key Characteristics of Least Privilege Enforcement:

- Identity-aware: Each request must carry valid credentials (JWT, mTLS cert, API key).

- Scoped access: Tokens are evaluated for scopes, roles, and expiration.

- Resource-based: Access decisions are made based on endpoint, method, or tenant.

- Time-bound: Sessions and tokens have short lifespans and explicit revocation paths.

- Adaptive enforcement: More sensitive APIs may require stronger auth (e.g., re-auth challenge).

API gateways, such as Kong, Apigee, AWS API Gateway, or Envoy, can enforce these rules at the first point of entry—meaning invalid, over-scoped, or expired requests never touch your services.

Example:

A token with the following scope:

json

CopyEdit

```
"scopes": ["read:products"]
```

Should not be able to:

- Call POST /products

- Access /orders

A Zero Trust-compliant gateway verifies this before routing.

Policy Enforcement Points (PEPs)

In Zero Trust models, gateways act as PEPs — intercepting traffic and applying authentication, authorization, and audit logic. They interact with centralized Policy Decision Points (PDPs) like OPA (Open Policy Agent), Okta, or Keycloak to retrieve access decisions in real-time.

9.2 JWT Validation at the Edge

JSON Web Tokens (JWT) are the de facto standard for stateless authentication in APIs. JWTs carry user identity, roles, expiration, and claims in a compact, signed format. But validation is non-trivial — and a misstep can compromise your entire system.

By validating JWTs at the gateway, you eliminate the burden on downstream services and enforce a single, hardened validation path.

JWT Validation Steps at the Gateway:

1. Extract token from the Authorization header:
   Authorization: Bearer <token>

2. Verify signature using public key or JWK endpoint.

3. Validate expiration (exp), audience (aud), and issuer (iss).

4. Check custom claims like role, scope, or tenant_id.

5. Inject trusted headers (e.g., x-user-id, x-scope) downstream.

Why Validate at the Edge?

- Reduces CPU overhead on microservices.

- Ensures consistent enforcement across all APIs.

- Enables caching and observability.

- Prevents bad actors from reaching business logic layers.

Example: Kong JWT Plugin

yaml

CopyEdit

```yaml
plugins:
  - name: jwt
    config:
      key_claim_name: "kid"
      secret_is_base64: false
      claims_to_verify: ["exp", "nbf"]
```

Once validated, the gateway adds headers:

http

CopyEdit

```http
x-consumer-id: 12345
x-scope: read:products
```

Microservices trust these headers (ideally, in a signed format or behind a private network).

9.3 OAuth2 Authorization Flows

Modern APIs rarely rely on static credentials. Instead, they integrate with OAuth2 providers (like Okta, Auth0, Google, or AWS Cognito) to manage authentication and delegation of access.

Gateways often handle OAuth2 flows directly — especially the token validation and enforcement part.

Common OAuth2 Flows Used at the Gateway:

1. Client Credentials Flow

Used for machine-to-machine APIs. The gateway checks:

- Client ID and secret

- Scopes embedded in the token

- Token expiration

2. Authorization Code Flow

Used for user-facing apps. The user logs in via a redirect flow, gets a token, and sends it in API requests.

The gateway:

- Validates the token with the identity provider

- Enforces scopes and roles

- Optionally introspects token against the /userinfo or /introspect endpoint

3. Token Introspection

For opaque tokens, the gateway queries the authorization server:

http

CopyEdit

POST /introspect

Authorization: Basic <client-creds>

Body: token=<access_token>

If the response includes "active": true, the gateway proceeds. Otherwise, it blocks.

4. Token Caching

To avoid hitting the IdP for every request, the gateway can cache valid tokens briefly (e.g., 60s), balancing performance with real-time control.

Example: Envoy + OAuth2 Filter

You can use Envoy's ext_authz filter to offload OAuth2 to an external authorization server like Keycloak or OPA, responding with headers or HTTP decisions.

9.4 Mutual TLS Authentication

While token-based auth secures API endpoints for external consumers, internal services — especially across zero-trust microservice boundaries — need stronger, certificate-based identity.

Mutual TLS (mTLS) ensures both the client and server authenticate each other using TLS certificates. This is particularly important in:

- Service-to-service communication

- API calls from trusted infrastructure

- Compliance-driven sectors (finance, healthcare)

How mTLS Works:

1. API gateway requests client certificate during TLS handshake.

2. Client presents a valid X.509 certificate.

3. Gateway verifies it against a trusted CA.

4. If valid, request proceeds; otherwise, rejected.

Benefits:

- Stronger than token-only auth — cryptographic identity at the transport layer.

- Certificate revocation and expiration enable tight security controls.

- No token replay attacks since certificates are per-session and harder to steal.

Example: AWS API Gateway + mTLS

json

CopyEdit

```json
"mutualTlsAuthentication": {
  "truststoreUri": "s3://mtls-bucket/cert.pem"
}
```

API Gateway will only accept requests with client certs issued by the CA in cert.pem.

In Kubernetes:

- Use Istio or Linkerd with mTLS enabled by default.

- All services have their own certificates issued by internal CA (e.g., cert-manager + Vault).

Design Best Practices:

- Rotate certificates frequently using automation.

- Use short-lived certs (e.g., 24–48h).

- Monitor for handshake failures and expired certs.

- Use separate CAs for different trust domains (e.g., prod vs staging).

9.5 Example: API Gateway with Okta and OAuth2

Let's walk through a real-world example where an API gateway integrates with Okta using OAuth2 and JWT validation — securing access to a product catalog service.

Goal:

- Only users with read:products scope can call /products

- Gateway validates token and injects user info downstream

- Unauthorized users are blocked at the edge

Step 1: Set Up Okta

- Register a new application (OAuth2 Service)

- Enable Client Credentials Flow

- Assign scopes (e.g., read:products, write:products)

- Get Client ID and Secret

Step 2: Get Access Token

bash

CopyEdit

```bash
curl --request POST \
  --url https://dev-xxxx.okta.com/oauth2/default/v1/token \
  --header 'Authorization: Basic <Base64(client_id:client_secret)>' \
  --header 'Content-Type: application/x-www-form-urlencoded' \
  --data 'grant_type=client_credentials&scope=read:products'
```

Step 3: Configure Gateway (Kong or Apigee)

Enable JWT plugin and point it to Okta's JWKs endpoint:

yaml

CopyEdit

```yaml
plugins:
  - name: jwt
    config:
      uri_param_names: ["token"]
      secret_is_base64: false
```

```
key_claim_name: "kid"

jwks_uri: "https://dev-xxxx.okta.com/oauth2/default/v1/keys"
```

Step 4: Inject User Identity

After validation, gateway adds:

http

CopyEdit

```
x-user-sub: 00u1234

x-user-scope: read:products
```

Your microservice can:

- Check x-user-scope

- Map x-user-sub to internal user ID

- Avoid repeating token validation logic

Step 5: Test

Make a request:

bash

CopyEdit

```
curl -H "Authorization: Bearer <access_token>" \
```

 https://api.example.com/products

Response:

json

CopyEdit

```
[

  { "id": 1, "name": "Widget A", "price": 9.99 }

]
```


Invalid token? Gateway returns:

json

CopyEdit

```
{

  "error": "unauthorized",

  "message": "JWT signature verification failed"

}
```


This model demonstrates how an API gateway:

- Acts as security enforcer

- Integrates identity providers

- Delivers zero trust principles in real traffic

Closing Thoughts on Zero Trust Gateway Security Patterns

Gateways are no longer just reverse proxies — they are policy enforcement engines for Zero Trust. By pushing authentication, authorization, and identity validation to the gateway layer, you reduce risk, improve scalability, and gain fine-grained control over access.

In a Zero Trust architecture, the API gateway becomes the guardrail between exposure and security:

- Verifying who is calling

- Controlling what they can access

- Monitoring how they behave

With gateways enforcing JWTs, OAuth2 scopes, and mTLS identities, you build systems that are not just scalable — they are secure by design.

PART III — Implementing with Major Cloud Providers

While design patterns provide the architectural blueprint, their true power is unlocked only when applied to real-world platforms. In this part of the book, we transition from theory to practice — demonstrating how major cloud providers implement and extend API gateway patterns within their ecosystems.

Each cloud provider — AWS, Azure, GCP, and others — offers unique capabilities, limitations, and operational models for API management. Yet they all serve the same core function: controlling, securing, routing, and scaling API traffic across distributed systems.

What distinguishes one provider from another isn't just tooling — it's how deeply the API gateway integrates with native services like identity management, observability stacks, CI/CD pipelines, and service meshes.

In this part, we will:

- Explore native gateway solutions like AWS API Gateway, Azure API Management, and GCP's API Gateway & Cloud Endpoints.

- Implement core patterns like canary releases, JWT validation, caching, throttling, and authentication using provider-native tools.

- Walk through production-grade deployment models, including serverless, container-based, and hybrid API strategies.

- Connect gateways to IAM services, serverless backends, load balancers, and observability tools — enabling a full-stack API control plane.

By the end of this section, you'll have the clarity and technical grounding to:

- Choose the right gateway for your use case

- Automate deployments using IaC (Terraform, ARM, CloudFormation)

- Monitor and secure APIs at scale in your cloud of choice

This is where your cloud-native API architecture takes real shape — not in whiteboards, but in working infrastructure.

Chapter 10: AWS API Gateway Design Patterns

10.1 REST vs HTTP vs WebSocket APIs

Amazon API Gateway offers three distinct API types — REST, HTTP, and WebSocket — each designed for specific use cases, protocols, and integration patterns. Understanding when and how to use each is foundational to designing robust architectures on AWS.

1. REST APIs

The original API Gateway offering, REST APIs are:

- Feature-rich and deeply integrated with AWS IAM, Cognito, API keys, usage plans.

- Ideal for enterprise-scale APIs with multiple stages, models, and throttling.

- Support fine-grained resource definitions and custom authorizers.

Use REST APIs when:

- You need API keys or detailed quota control.

- You're implementing multi-tenant APIs with complex resource trees.

- Deep integration with AWS service proxy (e.g., calling DynamoDB directly).

2. HTTP APIs

Released later, HTTP APIs are:

- Lightweight and cost-efficient.

- Lower latency and simpler configuration.

- Perfect for most modern serverless workloads.

Use HTTP APIs when:

- Building Lambda-backed services.

- Integrating with ALB, Step Functions, or external URLs.

- You want a simplified experience with OAuth2/JWT authorizers.

Key tradeoff: HTTP APIs support only a subset of features from REST APIs but at a lower price and complexity.

3. WebSocket APIs

These are designed for real-time, two-way communication:

- Ideal for chat apps, dashboards, live metrics, IoT communication.

- Routes are defined as message types (e.g., $connect, $disconnect, sendMessage).

- Backed by Lambda or other AWS services via integration.

Use WebSocket APIs when:

- You need persistent, bidirectional connections.

- You're building live updates, collaboration tools, or device communication layers.

Choosing Between Them:

Feature	REST API	HTTP API	WebSocket API
Cost	$$$	$	$$
Latency	Higher	Lower	Streaming
IAM Integration	Full	Limited	Partial
Caching	☑	✖	✖
Authorizers	Custom, Cognito	JWT, Cognito	Lambda only
Real-time Support	✖	✖	☑

The type of API you choose fundamentally affects cost, scalability, and maintainability — design accordingly from the start.

10.2 Lambda Proxy Integration

Lambda Proxy Integration is the most common and powerful pattern used with AWS API Gateway — especially in serverless architectures. It turns the gateway into a lightweight router and shifts business logic into Lambda functions.

What is Lambda Proxy Integration?

In this mode, the entire HTTP request — including path, headers, body, method, query string — is passed directly to the Lambda function. The function returns a standard structure:

json

CopyEdit

```
{
  "statusCode": 200,
  "headers": { "Content-Type": "application/json" },
  "body": "{\"message\": \"Hello World\"}"
}
```

This gives developers full control over:

- Routing logic

- Input validation

- Authentication responses

- Dynamic content generation

Benefits:

- No need to define individual resources or methods in the gateway

- Flexible, scalable, and works well with frameworks like Express (via AWS Lambda adapters)

- Clean separation between API interface and backend logic

Considerations:

- You must handle routing, validation, and response shaping in your code.

- If not optimized, cold starts or poor function design can lead to latency.

Best Practices:

- Use lightweight Lambda runtimes (Node.js, Go) for low latency.

- Minimize dependencies and cold start overhead.

- Pre-validate and parse inputs using libraries like ajv, zod, or pydantic.

10.3 Authorizers and Custom Domain Mapping

To build secure, production-grade APIs on AWS, two essential configurations are Authorizers and Custom Domains.

Authorizers

Authorizers let you validate incoming requests before they reach your backend —
enforcing security at the edge.

Types:

1. Lambda Authorizers (Custom)

   - Custom logic (e.g., call to third-party OAuth2 provider, database token
     checks)

   - Return IAM policy: allow/deny + context

2. JWT Authorizers

   - Built-in support in HTTP APIs

   - Validate tokens issued by providers like Cognito, Auth0, Okta

   - Map claims to route access

Example:

json

CopyEdit

```
{
  "sub": "user123",
```

```
    "scope": "read:products"

}
```

Gateways inspect this before passing the request to Lambda.

Use Cases:

- Multi-tenant access control

- Role-based feature toggles

- Per-user API quotas

Custom Domain Mapping

Production APIs need branded, secure URLs, not AWS-managed domains like xyz.execute-api.region.amazonaws.com.

With custom domains, you can:

- Map /api or /v1/* to different stages

- Use SSL via ACM (AWS Certificate Manager)

- Route requests with API Gateway base path mappings

Example:

plaintext

CopyEdit

CopyEdit

api.mycompany.com/v1 → API Gateway (prod stage)

api.mycompany.com/dev → API Gateway (dev stage)

This setup is essential for CI/CD workflows, client SDK generation, and SEO compliance.

10.4 Deployment with Terraform and SAM

Infrastructure as Code (IaC) ensures repeatable, version-controlled deployments of your API infrastructure. AWS supports multiple frameworks, but two dominate the serverless space: Terraform and SAM (Serverless Application Model).

Terraform for API Gateway

Terraform provides complete control over API Gateway, Lambda, IAM, and more.

Example:

hcl

CopyEdit

```
resource "aws_api_gateway_rest_api" "myapi" {
  name = "MyAPI"
}
```

```
resource "aws_api_gateway_resource" "product" {

  rest_api_id = aws_api_gateway_rest_api.myapi.id

  parent_id  = aws_api_gateway_rest_api.myapi.root_resource_id

  path_part  = "products"

}


resource "aws_lambda_function" "handler" {

  filename      = "function.zip"

  function_name = "handler"

  handler       = "index.handler"

  runtime       = "nodejs18.x"

  role          = aws_iam_role.lambda_exec.arn

}
```

Terraform excels in multi-region, multi-team deployments, and integrates with CI/CD pipelines via GitHub Actions, CodePipeline, or Jenkins.

AWS SAM

SAM is AWS-native and great for serverless-first projects.

Example template.yaml:

```yaml
```

CopyEdit

```yaml
Resources:
  ProductsApi:
    Type: AWS::Serverless::Api
    Properties:
      StageName: prod

  GetProductsFunction:
    Type: AWS::Serverless::Function
    Properties:
      Handler: index.handler
      Runtime: nodejs18.x
      Events:
        Products:
          Type: Api
          Properties:
            Path: /products
            Method: get
```

SAM CLI lets you:

- Build and test locally (sam local start-api)

- Deploy (sam deploy)

- Package (sam package)

It's ideal for fast iterations and developer-centric workflows.

10.5 Real-World Use Case: Serverless App Gateway

Let's build a simplified serverless e-commerce product catalog API with API Gateway, Lambda, and DynamoDB.

Architecture:

plaintext

CopyEdit

Client → API Gateway → Lambda → DynamoDB

     ↘ CloudWatch Logs

Use Case:

- GET /products — list all products

- GET /products/{id} — get details

- POST /products — add product (secured with JWT)

Step 1: Define API in API Gateway (HTTP API)

json

CopyEdit

```json
{
  "routes": [
    { "path": "/products", "method": "GET" },
    { "path": "/products/{id}", "method": "GET" },
    { "path": "/products", "method": "POST", "authorizer": "jwt" }
  ]
}
```

Step 2: Lambda Function (Node.js)

js

CopyEdit

```js
exports.handler = async (event) => {

  if (event.requestContext.http.method === 'GET') {

    // Return list or product by ID

  } else if (event.requestContext.http.method === 'POST') {

    // Validate JWT claims, write to DynamoDB

  }

};
```

Step 3: JWT Authorizer (Cognito or Auth0)

- Register app, define scopes (e.g., admin:create)

- Gateway validates token, passes claims in header

- Lambda checks scope before writing

Step 4: Observe and Monitor

- Use CloudWatch Logs for function tracing

- Set up API Gateway metrics: latency, 4xx/5xx

- Enable X-Ray tracing for end-to-end visibility

Benefits Realized:

- Fast deployment

- Secure endpoints

- Fully managed, auto-scaling

- Observability out of the box

This model powers many real-world apps — from startups to large-scale consumer APIs.

Closing Thoughts on AWS API Gateway Design Patterns

AWS API Gateway is more than a routing layer — it's a central hub for building, securing, and scaling APIs in the cloud. Whether you're building RESTful microservices, real-time apps, or high-throughput public endpoints, API Gateway integrates seamlessly with the AWS ecosystem.

By combining:

- The right API type (REST/HTTP/WebSocket)

- Strong identity enforcement (JWT, Lambda authorizers)

- IaC with Terraform or SAM

- Cloud-native services like Lambda, DynamoDB, Cognito

You gain an operationally mature API infrastructure that adapts with your product.

Chapter 11: Azure API Management Gateway Architecture

11.1 API Products, Policies, and Scopes

Azure API Management (APIM) is Microsoft's enterprise-grade platform for creating consistent and modern API gateways across internal services, external partners, and consumer-facing apps. At its heart is a philosophy of governed exposure — every API is wrapped in a gateway with structured products, policies, and access scopes.

API Products

A Product in APIM is a logical grouping of APIs — used to manage access, visibility, and consumption plans. Products can be:

- Public — discoverable by anyone via the Developer Portal

- Protected — requiring subscriptions and approval

- Private — only available to specific groups or users

Each product may include:

- One or more APIs

- Rate limits and quotas

- Required approvals for subscription

- Documentation and terms of use

Use Cases:

- A "Free Tier" product with low quota and rate limits

- A "Premium" product offering higher limits and SLA-backed endpoints

- A "Partner Only" product gated behind approval workflows

API Scopes

Scopes define permission boundaries. You can bind specific scopes to endpoints to control what clients can access after they authenticate using OAuth2 or OpenID Connect.

Example:

- scope: orders.read grants access to GET /orders

- scope: orders.write is required for POST /orders

These scopes align with Azure Active Directory (AAD) or custom identity providers, enforcing least-privilege principles across APIs.

Policies

Policies are the most powerful feature of APIM. These are XML-based configurations that allow you to customize the behavior of the gateway — without changing backend code.

Categories of Policies:

- Inbound: Executed before the request hits the backend

- Backend: Configure calls to the backend service

- Outbound: Modify the response before returning to the client

- On-error: Handle exceptions and timeouts

Common Examples:

xml
CopyEdit

```
<inbound>
  <validate-jwt header-name="Authorization" require-scheme="Bearer">
    <openid-config
url="https://login.microsoftonline.com/tenant/v2.0/.well-known/openid-configuration"
/>
    <required-claims>
      <claim name="scp">
        <value>read:products</value>
      </claim>
    </required-claims>
  </validate-jwt>
</inbound>
```

You can also:

- Transform payloads (XML $\leftrightarrow$ JSON)

- Set CORS headers

- Mask or inject fields

- Call external services (chained API calls)

These declarative policies let you enforce enterprise-grade security and data handling rules at the edge.

11.2 Managing Access and Throttling

APIM provides robust tools to control who can access your APIs, how frequently, and under what conditions.

Access Management

APIM supports:

- Subscription keys (per user/app) — used to track, throttle, and bill usage

- OAuth2 tokens — with built-in validation for AAD, Auth0, Okta, etc.

- IP whitelisting and caller restrictions

- Groups — to segment access (developers, admins, external partners)

Each developer, product, or app must subscribe to a product to gain access. Subscriptions are managed securely through:

- Manual approval flows

- Expiry dates

- Revocation mechanisms

Rate Limiting & Quotas

To prevent abuse and ensure fair use of APIs, APIM supports per-subscription limits via policies:

- Rate Limiting (requests per second/minute)

- Quota Enforcement (total requests or bandwidth per day/month)

- Burst Control (spike buffering)

Example:

xml
CopyEdit

```xml
<rate-limit-by-key calls="100" renewal-period="60"
increment-condition="@(context.Request.Headers.GetValueOrDefault("x-client-id") !=
null)" />
<quota-by-key calls="1000" renewal-period="86400" />
```

This ensures:

- Fair usage across clients

- Predictable backend load

- Billing models for monetized APIs

Tip: Use x-client-id or x-subscription-id as partition keys for granular enforcement.

11.3 Developer Portal and API Lifecycle

Azure APIM includes a built-in Developer Portal that allows external consumers, partners, and internal teams to:

- Discover APIs and their documentation

- Register and manage their own applications

- Retrieve keys and tokens

- Try APIs via Swagger-enabled testing UI

- Monitor usage and quotas

Customization

The portal is fully customizable via a WYSIWYG editor and supports:

- Branding (logo, colors, layout)

- Markdown docs and code samples

- Role-based access (anonymous, registered, or admin users)

You can even integrate analytics dashboards for client-side reporting.

API Lifecycle Management

APIM provides native tooling to manage the full lifecycle:

- Versioning: Segment APIs as v1, v2, etc. via path, header, or query string

- Revisions: Test changes to APIs without affecting consumers

- Deprecation Notices: Notify developers when a version is about to be sunset

- Documentation: Use OpenAPI (Swagger) definitions and policies to auto-generate docs

This aligns with CI/CD principles — you version, revise, and publish APIs without downtime or consumer confusion.

11.4 Hybrid Deployments

Azure APIM supports hybrid gateway architecture, allowing you to run gateways:

- In the cloud (fully managed)

- On-premises (via Docker containers)

- At the edge (inside Kubernetes, IoT environments)

This model enables:

- Data sovereignty compliance (run APIs in a country or region)

- Latency reduction (gateways closer to the consumer)

- Offline operation (gateway available even during cloud outages)

- Service mesh integration (inject API control into local networks)

Self-Hosted Gateway

- A containerized version of the APIM gateway

- Authenticates with the Azure cloud but processes requests locally

- Works with Kubernetes (Helm charts) and Docker Swarm

Example Use Case:
 A healthcare provider needs to expose APIs in hospitals with no internet access but still maintain central visibility and policy control.

The hybrid model allows Azure to serve as a control plane, while the local gateway acts as the data plane — enforcing policies, caching, logging, and rate-limiting independently.

11.5 CI/CD with Azure DevOps Pipelines

Operationalizing APIM means managing APIs, policies, and configurations as code. Azure DevOps Pipelines provides robust CI/CD tooling to automate:

- API imports from OpenAPI specs

- Product creation and versioning

- Policy deployment (XML or ARM templates)

- Environment-specific configurations (dev, stage, prod)

Pipeline Stages

1. Validate API Specs:

    ○ Lint and test OpenAPI definitions.

2. Deploy Infrastructure:

    ○ Use ARM or Bicep templates to deploy APIM instances.

3. Push API Definitions:

    ○ Use az apim api import or REST API to deploy/update APIs.

4. Apply Policies and Products:

    o   Upload policy.xml files for each route or operation.

5. Smoke Test APIs:

    o   Use Postman or REST-assured to verify deployments.

Example YAML Snippet:

yaml

CopyEdit

```
steps:
  - task: AzureCLI@2
    inputs:
      azureSubscription: 'my-connection'
      scriptType: 'bash'
      scriptLocation: 'inlineScript'
      inlineScript: |
        az apim api import \
          --service-name my-apim \
          --resource-group rg1 \
          --path orders \
          --api-id orders-api \
          --specification-format OpenApi \
          --specification-path openapi.yaml
```

Key Benefits:

- Full traceability of API changes

- Rapid rollback in case of errors

- Environment parity across dev, staging, and production

This approach makes API deployment just another component of your software delivery pipeline, integrating API lifecycle directly into DevOps workflows.

Closing Thoughts on Azure API Management Gateway Architecture

Azure API Management offers a comprehensive platform for designing, securing, scaling, and monitoring APIs. It's more than a reverse proxy — it's a policy engine, lifecycle manager, developer hub, and hybrid gateway controller rolled into one.

By leveraging:

- Products and scopes for access governance

- Policies for secure request manipulation

- Developer Portal for easy onboarding

- CI/CD pipelines for automation

- Hybrid architecture for compliance and reach

...you build APIs that are secure by default, operationally repeatable, and business-aligned.

Chapter 12: Google Cloud API Gateway and Apigee

12.1 GCP Cloud Endpoints

Google Cloud Endpoints is a lightweight API management solution built directly on Google Cloud infrastructure. It allows you to expose and control APIs backed by:

- Cloud Functions

- Cloud Run

- App Engine

- GKE (Kubernetes)

- Any backend on HTTP(S)

Endpoints acts as a reverse proxy, protecting your services while enforcing authentication, logging, and monitoring.

Key Features:

- OpenAPI and gRPC support: Define your API with OpenAPI 2/3 or Protocol Buffers.

- API Key Management: Restrict access via API keys and usage quotas.

- Authentication: Validate tokens issued by Firebase Auth, Google OAuth2, or custom IdPs.

- Monitoring: Integrated with Cloud Monitoring, Trace, and Logging.

- Performance: Low-latency edge proxy via ESP (Extensible Service Proxy).

How It Works:

1. You deploy your backend (Cloud Run, GKE, etc.).

2. Deploy ESPv2 sidecar or proxy in front of it.

3. The proxy validates requests, enforces auth policies, and logs telemetry.

4. Only valid requests are forwarded to the backend.

Use Case:

Expose a serverless REST API on Cloud Run that:

- Validates Firebase tokens

- Limits traffic to 1,000 reqs/day per key

- Logs metrics to Cloud Monitoring

Example OpenAPI Definition:
yaml

CopyEdit

swagger: "2.0"
info:
  title: My API
  version: "1.0.0"
host: my-api.endpoints.my-project.cloud.goog
x-google-endpoints:
  - name: my-api.endpoints.my-project.cloud.goog
    allowCors: true
securityDefinitions:
  firebase:
    authorizationUrl: ""
    flow: "implicit"
    type: "oauth2"
    x-google-issuer: "https://securetoken.google.com/my-project"
    x-google-jwks_uri:
"https://www.googleapis.com/service_accounts/v1/jwk/securetoken@system.gserviceac
count.com"
    x-google-audiences: "my-project"

12.2 Apigee Architecture and Key Features

For enterprise-grade needs, Apigee is Google Cloud's advanced API management platform. It offers full lifecycle capabilities: from design and versioning to monetization, analytics, and multi-cloud gateway deployment.

Core Components:

159

- API Proxies: Abstract and protect backend services behind a stable interface.

- Policies: Reusable logic (e.g., rate limiting, transformation, auth) applied without touching code.

- Developer Portal: Self-service access for developers and partners.

- Analytics: In-depth reporting on traffic, errors, latency, and custom events.

- Monetization: Define and bill usage plans for external API consumers.

Apigee Deployment Models:

1. Apigee X: Fully integrated with Google Cloud.

2. Apigee Hybrid: Control plane in GCP, runtime on GKE or on-prem.

3. Apigee Edge (legacy): Hosted in Apigee-managed infra.

Apigee supports both low-code configuration via its UI and declarative API deployment via apigeecli, Terraform, and APIs.

Key Advantages:

- Built-in OAuth2, API Key, JWT verification.

- Policy chaining: Modular XML-based policies for routing, transformation, mediation.

- Native support for GraphQL, SOAP, and REST.

- Powerful role-based access control and multi-tenancy.

12.3 Policy Configuration and Quotas

Apigee shines in its policy engine, which allows you to layer cross-cutting concerns (e.g., auth, rate limiting, transformation) on top of your APIs — declaratively, without rewriting code.

Common Policy Types:

- Authentication: API Key, OAuth2, JWT, mTLS

- Traffic Control: Spike arrest, concurrent call limits, quotas

- Mediation: XML/JSON transformation, SOAP to REST bridging

- Security: Threat protection, CORS, header sanitization

- Custom Logic: JavaScript, Python, and Java support

Example: Quota Policy

xml

CopyEdit

```
<Quota name="QuotaPerUser">
  <Allow count="1000"/>
  <Interval>1</Interval>
```

```xml
<TimeUnit>day</TimeUnit>
<Identifier ref="request.header.x-user-id"/>
</Quota>
```

This limits each user to 1,000 requests per day, based on a header.

Example: VerifyJWT Policy

xml

CopyEdit

```xml
<VerifyJWT name="VerifyAccessToken">
 <Algorithm>RS256</Algorithm>
 <PublicKey>
  <JWKS uri="https://auth.mycompany.com/.well-known/jwks.json"/>
 </PublicKey>
 <Subject>required</Subject>
 <Audience>my-api</Audience>
 <Issuer>https://auth.mycompany.com</Issuer>
</VerifyJWT>
```

This ensures that only valid JWTs issued by your IdP can access your proxy.

Quota Enforcement Strategies:

- Per app or API key

- Per developer

- Per IP address

- Based on headers or query params

Apigee supports fine-grained quota tracking, allowing product managers to define custom plans and monetization tiers.

12.4 Multi-Region Deployment

Enterprises often operate across multiple geographies and availability zones. Apigee supports multi-region, high-availability architectures that:

- Minimize latency to end users

- Provide failover in case of regional outages

- Meet compliance and data residency requirements

Deployment Strategies:

1. Active-Active:

   - Deploy runtime instances in multiple GCP regions

   - DNS-based load balancing with health checks

   - Session affinity or sticky routing if stateful

2. Active-Passive:

   o   Primary region handles traffic

   o   Secondary stands by, enabled only on failover

   o   Useful when minimizing costs or isolating traffic

3. Hybrid Model:

   o   Runtime runs on-premises or in other clouds

   o   Control plane stays managed by Apigee in GCP

   o   Used when integrating with legacy systems, data centers, or private cloud

Considerations:

- Replicate policies, products, and proxy definitions across regions.

- Use Google Cloud Load Balancing and Cloud Armor for global front-door.

- Monitor replication health via Apigee Analytics and Ops dashboards.

This flexibility makes Apigee suitable for global SaaS platforms, fintech applications, and regulated industries.

12.5 Deployment with gcloud and Terraform

Managing APIs manually is unsustainable at scale. Infrastructure as Code (IaC) tools like Terraform and the gcloud CLI allow repeatable, version-controlled API deployment on GCP.

Using gcloud for Endpoints:

Deploy an OpenAPI spec:

bash
CopyEdit

```
gcloud endpoints services deploy openapi.yaml
```

Enable your gateway:

bash
CopyEdit

```
gcloud run deploy my-service \
  --image gcr.io/my-project/image \
  --platform managed \
  --set-env-vars ESP_ENDPOINTS=my-api.endpoints.my-project.cloud.goog
```

Test with a valid token:

bash
CopyEdit

```
curl -H "Authorization: Bearer $TOKEN" \
  https://my-api.endpoints.my-project.cloud.goog/resource
```

Using Terraform with Apigee

Example: Deploy API Proxy and product

hcl

CopyEdit

```
resource "google_apigee_api_proxy" "orders" {
  org_id = "my-org-id"
  name   = "orders-api"
  bundle = "orders-api.zip"
}


resource "google_apigee_product" "premium" {
  name            = "PremiumProduct"
  display_name    = "Premium Tier"
  api_resources   = ["/orders/*"]
  environments    = ["prod"]
  quota           = 1000
  quota_interval  = "1"
  quota_time_unit = "day"
}
```

With terraform apply, you can deploy:

- Proxies

- Environments

- Developer apps

- Rate limits and API keys

CI/CD Integration:

- Use Cloud Build or GitHub Actions to deploy on merge

- Store OpenAPI definitions and proxy bundles in Git repos

- Automate key rotation, environment creation, and deployment testing

This level of automation supports enterprise-grade change management and allows teams to push API changes with confidence.

Closing Thoughts on Google Cloud API Gateway and Apigee

Google Cloud provides two powerful tracks for API management:

- Cloud Endpoints: Lightweight, fast, cost-effective — ideal for microservices and serverless apps.

- Apigee: Full-stack API management — ideal for enterprises needing security, monetization, hybrid control, and rich analytics.

Both integrate deeply with GCP's identity, observability, and DevOps ecosystems, letting you build modern APIs that are:

- Secure

- Scalable

- Globally available

- Operable across the full lifecycle

Whether you're exposing a Cloud Run function to partners or managing thousands of APIs for global mobile apps, Google's API platforms give you the building blocks to succeed.

Chapter 13: Kong, NGINX, and Open Source Gateways

13.1 Kong Gateway Design Patterns

Kong Gateway is one of the most widely adopted open-source API gateway solutions in the cloud-native ecosystem. Built on top of NGINX and OpenResty, it offers a robust plugin system, declarative configuration, and powerful routing and transformation features.

Core Capabilities:

- Plugin-driven architecture: auth, logging, rate limiting, transformations

- Native support for PostgreSQL or Cassandra as a config DB

- DB-less mode (declarative YAML files) for GitOps workflows

- Horizontal scalability with clustering

- RESTful Admin API for runtime management

Design Patterns:

1. Plugin Chaining:
   You can compose multiple plugins per route or service:

   - Auth → Rate Limiting → Caching → Logging

- All enforced at the gateway before request hits backend

Declarative Config via decK:

Use deck (Kong's IaC tool) to manage gateway state as versioned YAML:

bash

CopyEdit

deck sync --config kong.yaml

2. This enables GitOps-style CI/CD for routing and security changes.

3. Hybrid Mode:

Kong can run with a separate control plane and data plane:

- Control plane: Handles config updates

- Data plane: Executes traffic, runs plugins

- Useful in multi-region and edge scenarios

Service Abstraction:

Each backend becomes a "service", and each HTTP route maps to a service.

yaml

CopyEdit

```
services:
  - name: product-api
    url: http://products.internal:9000
routes:
```

```
- name: get-products
  paths: [/products]
  methods: [GET]
  service: product-api
```

Example Use Case:

- A mobile backend with JWT authentication, response caching, and usage logging

- Implemented entirely at the gateway layer, keeping microservices clean

Kong balances performance and flexibility with a strong plugin ecosystem and enterprise support (Kong Enterprise) when needed.

13.2 NGINX Ingress Controller in Kubernetes

In Kubernetes environments, the NGINX Ingress Controller is the de facto solution for exposing services to external traffic. While not a full API gateway in the traditional sense, it can be extended with annotations and ConfigMaps to replicate key gateway patterns.

Features:

- TLS termination

- URL-based routing

- Basic rate limiting, auth, and rewrites

- Configurable via annotations and custom templates

Example Ingress Resource:

yaml

CopyEdit

```yaml
apiVersion: networking.k8s.io/v1
kind: Ingress
metadata:
  name: app-ingress
  annotations:
    nginx.ingress.kubernetes.io/rewrite-target: /
    nginx.ingress.kubernetes.io/proxy-body-size: "10m"
spec:
  tls:
    - hosts:
        - api.mydomain.com
      secretName: tls-cert
  rules:
    - host: api.mydomain.com
      http:
        paths:
          - path: /products
            pathType: Prefix
            backend:
              service:
                name: product-service
                port:
                  number: 80
```

Advanced Features via Annotations:

Rate limiting:

yaml

CopyEdit

nginx.ingress.kubernetes.io/limit-rps: "10"

- Auth (e.g., basic auth, external auth server):

  yaml

  CopyEdit

  nginx.ingress.kubernetes.io/auth-url: "http://auth-service/validate"
- Limitations:
- No built-in support for JWT validation or dynamic plugin execution

- No centralized policy engine

- Scaling features depend heavily on Kubernetes-level autoscaling

Best Use:

For teams that want lightweight ingress control inside Kubernetes with full access to custom NGINX configuration.

13.3 API Gateway with Traefik and HAProxy

Traefik

Traefik is a modern reverse proxy and edge router built for dynamic container environments like Docker and Kubernetes.

Key Features:

- Dynamic service discovery

- Integrated Let's Encrypt support

- Dashboard and metrics

- Middleware: rate limiting, JWT validation, path rewrites

Why Use It:

- Dynamic environments (auto-updates routes as containers scale)

- Easily integrates with Docker Swarm, Kubernetes, ECS, Nomad

Example Configuration (Kubernetes IngressRoute):

yaml
CopyEdit

```
apiVersion: traefik.containo.us/v1alpha1
kind: IngressRoute
metadata:
 name: products-route
spec:
 entryPoints:
  - websecure
```

```yaml
routes:
  - match: PathPrefix(`/products`)
    kind: Rule
    services:
      - name: product-service
        port: 80
  tls:
    certResolver: myresolver
```

Middlewares:

yaml

CopyEdit

```yaml
rateLimit:
  average: 100
  burst: 20
```

Traefik shines in dev-friendly setups where agility, auto-discovery, and integrated HTTPS matter more than fine-grained policy control.

HAProxy

HAProxy is an extremely fast, reliable reverse proxy and load balancer that can also be extended as a high-performance gateway.

Key Advantages:

- Native support for L7 routing and SSL termination

- Lua scripting for custom logic (e.g., JWT validation)

- Proven track record in performance-critical applications

- Widely used in fintech, gaming, and telco workloads

HAProxy Gateway Pattern:

- Central TLS termination

- Routing by path, header, method

- Lua-based extensions for token validation or response transforms

Example (Simplified):

haproxy
CopyEdit

```
frontend api
  bind *:443 ssl crt /cert.pem
  http-request set-header X-Request-ID %[req_id]
  acl is_products path_beg /products
  use_backend products_backend if is_products

backend products_backend
  server product1 10.0.0.1:8080
```

HAProxy is best suited when performance, control, and extensibility are top priorities — often in on-prem or hybrid cloud environments.

13.4 OpenResty and Lua Plugins

OpenResty is a powerful web platform built on top of NGINX and LuaJIT, enabling you to extend NGINX with custom logic using Lua scripts. It is the engine underneath Kong Gateway and enables low-latency execution of dynamic logic at the edge.

Why Lua?

- Executes natively within NGINX worker process (no external calls)

- Handles JSON, regex, crypto, and HTTP transformations efficiently

- Enables custom plugins: e.g., IP-based throttling, A/B routing, token validation

OpenResty Use Cases:

- Implementing JWT parsing and RBAC

- Building API analytics and audit trails

- Performing real-time payload sanitization

- Writing dynamic traffic shaping rules

Example: Lua for Token Introspection
lua
CopyEdit

```lua
local http = require "resty.http"
```

```
local token = ngx.var.http_authorization

local res = httpc:request_uri("https://idp.example.com/introspect", {
  method = "POST",
  body = "token=" .. token,
  headers = {
    ["Content-Type"] = "application/x-www-form-urlencoded"
  }
})
```

Tradeoffs:

- Extremely powerful, but requires Lua expertise

- Complex logic must be well-tested to avoid crashing NGINX workers

- No built-in package isolation (sandboxing must be enforced)

OpenResty is ideal when you need highly customized control and are building your own gateway logic — particularly in performance-sensitive or regulated industries.

13.5 Best Practices for Open Source Gateways in Production

Deploying open-source gateways in production environments requires rigorous planning around security, observability, scalability, and maintainability.

Security:

- Always terminate TLS at the gateway

- Validate input (headers, query params, payload size)

- Use JWT or mTLS for authentication where possible

- Rate-limit and throttle APIs to mitigate abuse

Observability:

- Integrate with Prometheus, Grafana, and ELK for:

    - Request metrics

    - Error rates

    - Latency breakdowns

- Trace requests using OpenTelemetry or Jaeger/Zipkin integrations

Configuration Management:

- Store gateway config in Git

- Use tools like decK (Kong), kustomize (K8s), or Ansible for config delivery

- Automate validation (linting, dry runs) in CI/CD pipelines

High Availability:

- Use health checks and active-passive failover where supported

- Run stateless gateway nodes behind a load balancer

- Use clustering or hybrid modes for dynamic config syncing

Plugin Governance:

- Vet open-source or community plugins for security risks

- Avoid plugin sprawl — standardize and reuse policy logic

- Where possible, write declarative policies over code-based logic

Resource Isolation:

- Run gateways in dedicated namespaces or clusters (especially with sensitive APIs)

- Monitor CPU/memory closely — plugin chains can grow unexpectedly expensive

- Apply network policies to restrict egress and ingress traffic

Closing Thoughts on Open Source Gateways

Open-source API gateways offer unparalleled flexibility and extensibility. From Kong's plugin-rich enterprise gateway, to the container-native simplicity of Traefik, the raw performance of HAProxy, and the programmable power of OpenResty, these tools give you full-stack control of your API edge.

When deployed thoughtfully, they deliver:

- High-performance traffic management

- Deep security enforcement

- Seamless integration with service meshes and CI/CD

- Full transparency and cost efficiency

But with that power comes responsibility — production-readiness demands a strong operational framework and team maturity.

PART IV — Security, Observability, and Automation

As modern API infrastructures grow in complexity, success hinges not only on scalable design but on how well you secure, monitor, and automate those systems. PART IV focuses on the operational maturity needed to run production-grade gateways in real-world environments.

This section explores how API gateways become active participants in Zero Trust enforcement, real-time observability, and DevSecOps automation — transforming them from simple traffic routers into dynamic control planes.

You'll learn how to:

- Implement end-to-end threat protection across layers (rate limiting, mTLS, token introspection)

- Build a telemetry-first architecture with tracing, logging, and performance dashboards

- Automate deployment, testing, rollback, and configuration via CI/CD

- Design for compliance, auditing, and incident response readiness

With a focus on practical tools and patterns — from JWT verification to OpenTelemetry, from GitOps to canary rollouts — this part helps you build gateways that are resilient, auditable, and operationally efficient.

Whether you're a platform engineer, architect, or API product lead, this section ensures you can scale securely, respond intelligently, and deploy fearlessly.

Chapter 14: Security Best Practices for API Gateways

14.1 Rate Limiting, Throttling, and Abuse Detection

Modern APIs are public-facing assets, often exposed to abuse, bot attacks, or unintentional overload. API gateways must therefore act as gatekeepers — not only routing traffic, but enforcing behavior constraints.

Rate Limiting vs Throttling

- Rate Limiting restricts the number of requests a client can make in a given time frame (e.g., 1,000 req/hour).

- Throttling controls request bursts — temporarily slowing down traffic without fully blocking it.

Most gateways — including Kong, Apigee, AWS API Gateway, and NGINX — support declarative rate-limiting policies based on:

- API key or token

- IP address

- Route or endpoint

- Authenticated user ID or tenant

Example (Kong Declarative Config):

yaml

CopyEdit

```yaml
plugins:
 - name: rate-limiting
   config:
     minute: 100
     policy: local
```

Abuse Detection Strategies:

- Track abnormal traffic patterns (e.g., high POST rate to login)

- Use behavior-based triggers (e.g., sudden spike in 429s)

- Correlate usage with identity and geolocation

- Alert or auto-block on indicators of scraping, credential stuffing, or replay attacks

Best Practices:

- Set rate limits per client class (free, premium, internal).

- Combine with IP reputation databases or fraud scoring APIs.

- Use analytics to continuously refine limits and thresholds.

14.2 IP Whitelisting and Geofencing

While identity-based access (OAuth2, JWT) is the norm, network-level access control remains a vital secondary defense — especially for internal APIs, back-office tools, or country-restricted endpoints.

IP Whitelisting:

Allow only trusted IPs or CIDR blocks:

- Used for private clients, partner apps, or internal services.

- Enforced via gateway access control plugins or infrastructure firewalls (e.g., AWS Security Groups).

Example (Apigee Policy):

xml
CopyEdit

```xml
<AccessControl>
  <IPRules include="true">
    <IP>192.168.1.0/24</IP>
    <IP>10.0.0.0/8</IP>
  </IPRules>
</AccessControl>
```

Geofencing:

Use IP geolocation databases to restrict access based on country or region.

- Useful for compliance (e.g., GDPR, ITAR) or market segmentation.

- Can be implemented at CDN, WAF, or gateway level.

Example (NGINX Geo Module):

nginx
CopyEdit
```
geoip_country /usr/share/GeoIP/GeoIP.dat;
if ($geoip_country_code != "US") {
  return 403;
}
```

Best Practices:

- Automate whitelisting for known services (e.g., CI/CD IPs).

- Use fail-safe deny-all policies with explicit allows.

- Periodically review and rotate allowlists.

- Pair with user-agent or API key verification for multi-layered access control.

14.3 Secrets Management and API Key Rotation

API gateways interact with numerous backend services, plugins, and identity providers — all of which require credentials: tokens, certificates, private keys, and API secrets.

Common Secrets Exposed in Gateways:

- JWT signing keys (HMAC or RSA)

- OAuth2 client secrets

- Backend service credentials

- TLS certificates

- API keys for third-party services (payment, analytics, etc.)

Best Practices for Secrets Management:

- Store secrets in dedicated secret managers, not hardcoded files or configs.

  - Examples: AWS Secrets Manager, Azure Key Vault, HashiCorp Vault, GCP Secret Manager

- Load secrets at runtime via environment variables, not embedded YAML.

- Enforce least privilege: only the gateway process should access the secret, scoped to the environment.

Key Rotation:

- Set expiration timelines for API keys and access tokens.

- Use rolling deployments to rotate secrets without downtime.

- Automate rotation via scheduled workflows or CI/CD jobs.

- Instruct client developers to gracefully handle key rollover events.

Tip: Track secrets usage via audit logs — revoke unused or leaked tokens immediately.

14.4 Web Application Firewall (WAF) Integration

A Web Application Firewall (WAF) provides an additional security layer that inspects and filters HTTP traffic based on known attack patterns. While API gateways focus on traffic flow and access control, WAFs are designed to detect and block:

- SQL injection attempts

- Cross-site scripting (XSS)

- XML/JSON payload anomalies

- Header manipulation

- OWASP Top 10 threats

How to Integrate a WAF:

- Place WAF in front of the API gateway (at the CDN or edge)

- Or embed WAF logic inside the gateway via plugins or filters

Options:

- Cloud WAFs: AWS WAF, Azure Front Door, Cloudflare WAF, Fastly

- Gateway Plugins: Kong plugin for ModSecurity, NGINX WAF modules

- Third-party WAF appliances: F5, Fortinet, Imperva

Example (AWS WAF rule to block XSS):

json
CopyEdit
```json
{
 "Rule": {
  "Name": "BlockXSS",
  "Statement": {
   "ByteMatchStatement": {
    "FieldToMatch": { "QueryString": {} },
    "SearchString": "<script>",
    "TextTransformations": [ { "Priority": 0, "Type": "URL_DECODE" } ]
   }
  },
  "Action": { "Block": {} }
 }
}
```

Best Practices:

- Use WAF in monitoring mode first, then enforce

- Regularly update rule sets

- Combine static rule sets with anomaly detection

- Include rate-based rules for bot mitigation

14.5 Common Security Pitfalls and How to Avoid Them

Even with sophisticated gateways, security breakdowns often stem from misconfiguration, overtrust, or lack of visibility. Here are some recurring mistakes and how to correct them:

- ◆ Misconfigured Authentication

  - Allowing anonymous access to sensitive endpoints

  - Using shared or long-lived tokens
    Fix: Enforce token validation at the gateway; rotate and expire tokens frequently.

- ◆ Missing Rate Limits

  - Unlimited access opens APIs to scraping, DDoS, or misuse
    Fix: Always set per-client rate limits; enforce burst control on login endpoints.

- Lack of TLS Enforcement

  - Serving APIs over HTTP or accepting plaintext traffic
    Fix: Enforce HTTPS-only traffic at the edge; use HSTS headers; validate certs in mutual TLS.

- Exposing Internal APIs

  - Accidentally exposing /admin, /debug, or internal service APIs
    Fix: Use path-based allow/deny rules; isolate sensitive APIs behind auth and IP filters.

- Poor Secret Hygiene

  - API keys embedded in codebases or config files
    Fix: Use environment variables or secret managers; rotate keys automatically.

- Insufficient Logging

  - No visibility into who accessed what and when
    Fix: Enable structured logging for request/response metadata; log token claims and trace IDs.

Conclusion

Security is not a feature — it's an operating posture. API gateways are your first line of defense, and by implementing layered security measures, enforcing principle of least privilege, and integrating with trusted identity and observability systems, you protect not just your APIs — but your business logic, customer data, and platform reputation.

Mastering security at the gateway means you catch threats before they hit your code, respond quickly to incidents, and build APIs that are resilient by design.

Chapter 15: Observability, Tracing, and Logging

15.1 Centralized Logging for Gateways

Logging is the foundation of observability. In distributed architectures, especially those powered by microservices and API gateways, it is critical to have centralized, structured, and queryable logs. Without them, debugging issues or investigating incidents becomes guesswork.

Why Centralized Logging Matters:

- Gateways touch every request — logs here are often the first point of insight into API behavior.

- Aggregating logs across gateways, backend services, and infrastructure provides full request visibility.

- Security and compliance audits rely on immutable, time-stamped logs.

Common Logging Layers in Gateways:

- Access Logs: IP, request path, method, status code, latency, request size.

- Auth Logs: JWT claims, scopes, token issuer.

- Error Logs: Backend errors, timeouts, rate limit violations, WAF denials.

- Plugin Logs: Rate limiting decisions, transformations, plugin execution trace.

Log Aggregation Tools:

- Cloud-native:

    - AWS CloudWatch Logs

    - Azure Monitor

    - Google Cloud Logging

- Open source:

    - ELK Stack (Elasticsearch, Logstash, Kibana)

    - Fluentd + Loki (Grafana)

    - Graylog, Vector

Example (Kong with Fluent Bit):

lua

CopyEdit

```lua
log_by_lua_block {
  local message = {
    client_ip = ngx.var.remote_addr,
    request = ngx.var.request_uri,
    status = ngx.status,
```

```
    latency = ngx.var.request_time,
    token_claims = ngx.var.jwt_claims or "unauthenticated"
  }
  ngx.log(ngx.INFO, cjson.encode(message))
}
```

Best Practices:

- Structure logs as JSON for easy parsing.

- Include correlation IDs (x-request-id) to trace across services.

- Mask sensitive fields like Authorization, Set-Cookie.

- Route all logs to a central destination, tagged by environment and service.

15.2 Distributed Tracing with OpenTelemetry

As microservices and gateways become more fragmented, traditional logs fall short in explaining request paths across systems. This is where distributed tracing comes in — letting you visualize and diagnose how a request moves through your architecture.

What Is OpenTelemetry?

OpenTelemetry (OTel) is the emerging standard for collecting:

- Traces: Request flow across services

- Metrics: Latency, errors, resource usage

- Logs: Contextual events

It works via instrumentation libraries and gateway agents, passing along trace context in HTTP headers.

Example: A Trace Through an API Gateway

1. Client makes request to GET /orders

2. Gateway logs span: request-received → policy-check → route-forward

3. Gateway forwards request with trace headers:

   - traceparent

   - x-b3-traceid, x-b3-spanid (for backward compatibility)

4. Backend services pick up trace and add spans

5. All spans are shipped to a tracing backend

Compatible Gateways:

- Kong: OpenTelemetry plugin

- Traefik: Native tracing support

- NGINX: Lua or OpenResty-based tracing libraries

- Apigee: Built-in integration with Stackdriver Trace

- Envoy: Native OTel support

Visualization Tools:

- Jaeger

- Zipkin

- Grafana Tempo

- AWS X-Ray

- GCP Cloud Trace

Best Practices:

- Always forward trace headers to downstream services

- Sample traces at ~1% in production (to avoid volume issues)

- Capture important labels: user ID, region, API route

- Use spans to measure plugin execution time (rate limiting, auth, etc.)

15.3 Prometheus, Grafana, and Metrics Exporters

Metrics allow you to understand system health at a glance. Gateways must expose real-time statistics like:

- Request volume

- Latency percentiles

- Error rates

- Status code distribution

- Rate limit counts

Prometheus Architecture:

- Scrapes metrics from exporters exposed by services (on /metrics endpoints)

- Stores time series data

- Can be queried with PromQL (e.g., rate(http_requests_total[5m]))

Gateway Integrations:

- Kong: prometheus plugin enables metrics export

- NGINX: nginx-prometheus-exporter parses access logs and metrics

- Traefik: Built-in Prometheus endpoint (:8080/metrics)

- Envoy: Native Prometheus output

- Apigee: Custom exporters required, or export to Stackdriver and bridge

Grafana Dashboards:

- Use dashboards to visualize:

    o Request rate over time

    o 4xx/5xx spikes

    o Latency histograms

    o Plugin error rates

    o Resource usage (CPU, memory)

Example Metric Snippet:

bash

CopyEdit

```
# HELP kong_http_requests_total Total number of HTTP requests
# TYPE kong_http_requests_total counter
kong_http_requests_total{service="products", status="200"} 12456
kong_http_requests_total{service="products", status="500"} 42
```

Best Practices:

- Define SLIs (e.g., "95% of requests under 200ms")

- Use recording rules to simplify repeated queries

- Alert on error budgets or saturation (e.g., latency > threshold)

15.4 Real-Time Monitoring and Alerts

Observability is incomplete without actionable, real-time alerting. Your gateway should detect and report anomalies as they happen — giving your team time to react before users are affected.

Key Monitoring Dimensions:

- Availability: Is the gateway reachable?

- Latency: Are responses taking longer than expected?

- Error rate: Are 5xx errors spiking?

- Traffic patterns: Sudden drops (crash) or spikes (DDoS)?

- Auth failures: Invalid tokens, expired credentials

Tooling:

- Prometheus Alertmanager

- Grafana Alerting

- Datadog

- New Relic

- Cloud-native tools (CloudWatch Alarms, Azure Monitor, Stackdriver Alerts)

Example Alert (PromQL):

promql
CopyEdit
rate(kong_http_requests_total{status=~"5.."}[5m]) > 5

"More than 5 server errors per minute → send Slack alert"

Alert Routing:

- PagerDuty (on-call)

- Slack/MS Teams (chat)

- Email/SMS (backup)

- Incident management tools (Opsgenie, VictorOps)

Best Practices:

- Define clear alert ownership

- Prioritize signal over noise (avoid alert fatigue)

- Set severity levels (info, warning, critical)

- Include playbooks in alerts (next steps, contact)

15.5 Dashboards and API Performance SLAs

Dashboards offer visibility across operations, development, and leadership — helping everyone see the health and value of your APIs.

Dashboard Categories:

1. Engineering Dashboards:

   o Request count per route

   o Plugin execution time

   o Backend response latency

   o 95th percentile latency over time

   o Traffic by region/user-agent

2. Product Dashboards:

    o API adoption trends

    o Active consumers

    o Quota consumption

    o New app onboarding rates

3. SLA Monitoring Dashboards:

    o Track contractual obligations:

        ▪ "99.9% availability"

        ▪ "<200ms median response time"

        ▪ "<1% error rate"

SLA Breach Example:

- If 95th percentile latency > 500ms for 3 days → dashboard shows red indicator

- Trigger automated email to account managers or service owners

Dashboard Tools:

- Grafana

- Google Looker Studio

- Power BI (for business KPIs)

- Kibana (for log-centric visuals)

Best Practices:

- Use templating and filters (e.g., per environment, service, region)

- Link dashboards to traces or logs for deep dive

- Version-control dashboard definitions for consistency across teams

- Keep dashboards visible and shared — operations is a team sport

---

Closing Thoughts on Observability, Tracing, and Logging

Modern API gateways must be more than traffic routers. They are critical observability nodes — surfacing the health, performance, and security of the entire service mesh they protect. By implementing structured logging, distributed tracing, and real-time metrics, you transform your gateway into an API command center — empowering faster resolution, better uptime, and richer insights.

When designed well, your observability stack becomes your first signal, not your last defense.

Chapter 16: CI/CD for API Gateway Deployments

16.1 GitOps and Infrastructure as Code

Modern software development isn't just about writing application code — it's about managing infrastructure, APIs, and security policies with the same rigor as software. This principle forms the basis of GitOps — using Git as the single source of truth for configuration, coupled with CI/CD to automate deployment.

What is GitOps?

GitOps applies DevOps practices to infrastructure and API management:

- All configurations live in Git (e.g., YAML files for APIs, routes, plugins).

- Changes are made via pull requests, reviewed and approved like code.

- Automation tools (CI/CD runners, Kubernetes controllers) observe Git and sync changes to production.

In API gateways, this includes:

- Route definitions

- Plugin configurations (rate limits, auth)

- Service mappings

- Traffic policies

- Custom error templates

Examples:

- Kong + decK: Git stores kong.yaml; deck sync applies to gateway.

- Apigee: Git stores API proxy bundles and environment configs; CI pipeline deploys via Apigee APIs.

- AWS API Gateway: Git manages SAM or CDK templates deployed via GitHub Actions or CodePipeline.

Benefits:

- Full audit trail

- Reproducible environments

- No manual drift or undocumented changes

- Built-in rollback via Git history

16.2 Versioning Strategies for APIs

APIs evolve. Keeping track of those changes — while maintaining backward compatibility and managing deployment risk — is one of the key responsibilities of gateway automation.

Common Versioning Approaches:

1. URI Versioning:

   o /v1/products, /v2/products

   o Clear separation; easy to manage in gateways

2. Header-Based:

   o Accept: application/vnd.company.product.v2+json

   o Keeps URL clean; requires client awareness

3. Query Parameter:

   o /products?version=2

   o Not ideal for REST principles; may confuse caching

In API Gateways:

- Each version maps to a separate route or proxy.

- Older versions can be depreciated gradually (e.g., log usage, notify developers, sunset date).

- Version metadata is included in:

  - OpenAPI spec files

  - Gateway config files

  - Developer portal documentation

Best Practices:

- Always keep at least two active versions (latest + one previous).

- Use semantic versioning for internal tracking.

- Ensure your CI pipeline validates spec compatibility before deployment.

16.3 Automated Testing for Gateways

Testing is essential for validating that API gateway configurations are correct and secure — especially when using automation.

Types of Tests:

1. Unit Tests (Linting & Schema):

- Validate YAML or JSON structure of config files

- Ensure OpenAPI definitions match required formats

2. Integration Tests:

    - Deploy changes to a staging gateway

    - Send HTTP requests to verify:

        - Routing

        - Plugin execution

        - Rate limiting

        - Auth policies

3. Contract Tests:

    - Use tools like Postman, Dredd, or Pact to validate expected request/response structures.

4. Security Tests:

    - Validate:

        - Endpoints are protected (401 if no auth)

- ■ Tokens are required and validated

- ■ CORS headers are correct

Example (GitHub Actions with Postman):

yaml

CopyEdit

```
- name: Run Postman Tests
  uses: matt-ball/newman-action@v1
  with:
    collection: ./tests/api-tests.postman_collection.json
    environment: ./tests/staging.postman_environment.json
```

Best Practices:

- Always test in a non-prod environment first

- Run tests on every pull request that touches gateway configs

- Include mock services if backend is not available

16.4 Canary and A/B Deployments with Pipelines

Modern deployments don't just "go live." They progressively deliver changes in controlled stages to reduce risk.

Canary Deployments

- Deploy new API version to a small percentage of traffic (e.g., 5%)

- Monitor for errors, latency, and regressions

- Gradually increase exposure until full rollout

Example (GCP Cloud Run + Traffic Splitting):

bash

CopyEdit

```
gcloud run services update-traffic my-api \
  --to-revisions revision1=90,revision2=10
```

Blue-Green Deployments

- Two environments: blue (current) and green (new)

- Deploy to green → test → switch traffic over

- Rollback = switch back to blue

A/B Testing

- Route users based on:

  - Cookies

  - Header values

- Random assignment (e.g., hash of IP)

- Used to test feature variants or performance improvements

Gateway Integration:

- Use plugins or route conditions:

  - Kong's traffic-splitting plugin

  - Apigee's conditional flows

  - NGINX Lua scripting for A/B logic

  - Istio/Envoy for weighted routing

Best Practices:

- Monitor real-time metrics during rollout

- Define rollback conditions (e.g., >5% error rate in 10 minutes)

- Automate rollback via CI/CD on failure signals

16.5 GitHub Actions, GitLab CI, and Bitbucket Pipelines

Your API gateway deployment process should be automated end-to-end using CI/CD pipelines. The right tooling depends on your team's Git platform.

GitHub Actions

- Declarative .yml files

- Native secrets and environment support

- Great for open source and cloud-native teams

Example: Kong Deployment with decK

yaml
CopyEdit

```
name: Deploy Kong Gateway
on:
  push:
    paths:
      - "kong/kong.yaml"

jobs:
  deploy:
    runs-on: ubuntu-latest
    steps:
      - uses: actions/checkout@v2
      - run: deck sync --config kong/kong.yaml
```

GitLab CI

- CI/CD tightly integrated with repo permissions

- Includes runners, environment dashboards, and protected branches

Example: Apigee Proxy Deployment

yaml

CopyEdit

```
deploy_proxies:
  script:
    - apigeetool deployproxy -n orders-api -e test -u $USERNAME -p $PASSWORD
```

Bitbucket Pipelines

- Integrated pipelines with YAML config

- Ideal for Atlassian users

- Supports containerized build steps and caching

Use Cases:

- AWS API Gateway deployments via Terraform

- Kong configuration sync

- NGINX ingress YAML updates via Helm or Kustomize

Closing Thoughts on CI/CD for API Gateway Deployments

A modern API architecture isn't just about powerful gateways — it's about repeatable, reliable, and safe delivery of changes. CI/CD ensures that updates to routes, security policies, plugins, and traffic shaping rules are versioned, tested, and deployed without human error.

By adopting:

- GitOps principles

- Full-lifecycle versioning

- Testing at multiple levels

- Progressive delivery strategies

- Seamless integration with your existing Git workflows

…your team builds an API infrastructure that is resilient, auditable, and responsive to change — without sacrificing velocity or safety.

Chapter 17: Resilience and Disaster Recovery

17.1 Failover Strategies and Health Checks

API gateways are mission-critical systems. If the gateway goes down, your entire API surface becomes unreachable, regardless of backend status. That's why robust failover and health check mechanisms are non-negotiable.

Key Concepts

- Failover is the automatic rerouting of traffic when a primary system fails.

- Health checks are periodic probes that determine the availability of services.

- Gateways must monitor both upstream (backend) and downstream (self) health.

Types of Health Checks:

1. Liveness Probe – Is the gateway process up?

2. Readiness Probe – Can the gateway accept traffic (DB connections, memory thresholds)?

3. Upstream Health – Are backends reachable and responding correctly?

Example (NGINX upstream health check):

nginx
CopyEdit
```
server backend1.example.com max_fails=3 fail_timeout=10s;
```

Failover Patterns:

- Passive Failover: Redirect traffic after detecting failure.

- Active-Active: Two or more gateways running simultaneously behind a load balancer.

- Active-Passive: Secondary system remains idle until failure occurs, then takes over.

Implementation Tips:

- Use load balancers (e.g., AWS ELB, Azure Front Door) to abstract health check logic.

- Keep gateway configuration stateless and replicable.

- Use container orchestrators (Kubernetes) to restart unhealthy pods automatically.

17.2 Geo-Redundancy and Multi-Region APIs

Geographic redundancy ensures availability and low latency across global regions, while also acting as a buffer against regional outages (e.g., cloud zone failure).

Goals:

- High availability across failure domains (AZs, regions)

- Data sovereignty compliance (keep traffic in-country)

- Latency optimization by routing to nearest region

Strategies:

1. DNS-Based Routing:

   o Use tools like AWS Route 53, Cloudflare, or NS1 to route traffic by geography or latency.

   o Define failover records with TTLs for quick switchovers.

2. Multi-Region API Deployment:

   o Deploy API gateways in multiple regions (e.g., us-east, eu-west).

   o Sync configurations using GitOps or service mesh control planes.

3. Data Replication:

- Use eventual consistency and read replicas across regions.

- Minimize write operations in multi-master setups unless absolutely needed.

Gateway Example (Apigee Hybrid):

- Control plane in GCP

- Data plane gateways in multiple GKE clusters (US, EU)

- Smart DNS to route traffic

Best Practices:

- Use active-active for read-heavy workloads

- Keep traffic regional when possible to avoid compliance issues

- Automate config sync across regions using pipelines or decK (for Kong)

17.3 Retry, Timeout, and Circuit Breaker Patterns

Building resilience also means gracefully handling transient failures without overloading systems or causing cascading downtime.

Retry Patterns

- Used for intermittent network failures or 5xx errors.

- Must include exponential backoff and jitter to prevent thundering herds.

Example (Kong plugin config):

yaml
CopyEdit
```
retries: 3
retry_timeout: 1000ms
```

Timeout Settings

- Define per-hop timeouts (client → gateway, gateway → backend).

- Prevent hanging requests that tie up system resources.

Example (NGINX config):

nginx
CopyEdit
```
proxy_connect_timeout 3s;
proxy_read_timeout 5s;
```

Circuit Breaker

- A protective mechanism that "trips" after repeated failures, temporarily stopping traffic to a failing service.

- Prevents overloading unhealthy services.

- Can be implemented in the gateway (via plugins) or service mesh.

Popular Tools:

- Envoy circuit breaker policy

- Hystrix, Resilience4j for Java services

- Istio and Linkerd for fine-grained policy enforcement

Example:

yaml

CopyEdit

```yaml
outlierDetection:
  consecutive5xxErrors: 5
  interval: 10s
  baseEjectionTime: 30s
```

Best Practices:

- Set timeouts conservatively

- Use retry budgets to avoid runaway retries

- Monitor retry/circuit metrics via Prometheus or Datadog

17.4 Traffic Steering with DNS and Load Balancers

Traffic control during incidents or planned migrations is critical. API gateways, combined with intelligent traffic steering, let you control how requests flow across clusters, regions, or service versions.

DNS Steering

- Latency-based: Send users to the closest region.

- Weighted routing: Gradually shift traffic (e.g., 90% old, 10% new).

- Failover routing: Route to standby on outage.

Tools:

- AWS Route 53 with health checks

- Cloudflare Load Balancing

- NS1 or Akamai for advanced geo-routing

Load Balancer Steering

- Use Layer 7 load balancers to route by path, hostname, headers.

- Example: Send /v2/orders to a different cluster.

Cloud Tools:

- AWS ALB for path/host routing

- Azure Application Gateway

- Google Cloud Load Balancer with URL maps

Canary Example Using DNS TTL:

- api.example.com has:

  - gateway-us-1 @ 80%

  - gateway-us-2 @ 20%

- Monitor latency and error rates

- Adjust weights gradually using CI/CD automation

17.5 Chaos Testing for Gateways

Chaos engineering helps validate that your system can withstand real-world failure scenarios — from node crashes to API rate surges. When applied to gateways, it strengthens both recovery readiness and confidence in failure tolerance.

Goals of Chaos Testing:

- Verify failover mechanisms (e.g., circuit breakers, retries)

- Confirm observability and alerting systems trigger as expected

- Discover unknown system dependencies and bottlenecks

Common Chaos Scenarios:

- Drop gateway pod or container mid-request

- Kill backend service and observe error propagation

- Simulate high latency or timeouts on one region

- Throttle upstream bandwidth

- Inject malformed traffic or spike auth failures

Tools:

- Gremlin: SaaS chaos platform

- Chaos Mesh (Kubernetes-native)

- Litmus: Declarative chaos testing for Kubernetes

- Custom scripts (e.g., tc for Linux network faults)

Example (Litmus Chaos Experiment):

yaml

CopyEdit

```yaml
apiVersion: litmuschaos.io/v1alpha1
kind: ChaosExperiment
metadata:
  name: pod-network-latency
spec:
  duration: '60'
  latency: '3000'
  targetPods:
    - app: kong-gateway
```

Best Practices:

- Run chaos tests in staging first

- Validate alerts, dashboards, auto-recovery behavior

- Always plan rollback and observability before injection

Closing Thoughts on Resilience and Disaster Recovery

In cloud-native architectures, resilience isn't a bonus — it's a requirement. Your API gateway must be engineered to withstand failure, handle traffic surges, and recover automatically when the unexpected happens.

By implementing:

- Health checks and failover automation

- Multi-region deployments

- Retry and circuit breaker logic

- Intelligent traffic steering

- Proactive chaos testing

…you build a system that not only recovers, but protects customer experience even when things break. Resilience is not about perfection — it's about control, observability, and repeatability in failure.

PART V — Advanced Scenarios and Real-World Architecture

In the final part of this book, we move beyond theoretical patterns and core gateway concepts to explore practical, real-world implementations across cloud platforms and enterprise environments. This section dives deep into the architectural decisions, trade-offs, and innovations that arise when building multi-cloud, hybrid, and compliance-driven API ecosystems at scale.

You'll explore:

- Complex deployments across AWS, Azure, and GCP

- How large organizations build multi-gateway strategies to isolate risk and optimize performance

- Case studies showing gateway integration with legacy systems, GraphQL, and event-driven backends

- Approaches to managing tenant isolation, policy enforcement, and cross-region consistency

Whether you're modernizing a monolith, running a global SaaS platform, or aligning with strict regulatory frameworks, the chapters ahead provide battle-tested blueprints to guide your next move.

This part is not just about best practices — it's about how real teams ship and scale API platforms under real constraints.

Chapter 18: Multi-Tenancy and Dynamic Routing

18.1 Routing Based on Headers, Path, or Tokens

In modern API architectures, especially multi-tenant environments, routing is rarely static. Instead, gateways must route requests dynamically — based on headers, path segments, or token claims — to the correct service, cluster, or configuration.

Dynamic Routing Dimensions:

- Path-Based:

  /tenant-a/api/v1/orders → Route to orders-service-a

  /tenant-b/api/v1/orders → Route to orders-service-b

- Header-Based:

  X-Tenant-ID: tenant-a

  X-Region: us-east

  → Gateway uses headers to determine service routing or apply tenant-specific policies.

- Token-Based (JWT/OAuth2 Claims):

  iss, sub, or custom claims identify the tenant

  Gateway decodes and uses this info to:

  - Lookup routing rules

  - Apply tenant-specific rate limits

o   Restrict access to certain APIs

Example: Kong Route with Header Matching

yaml

CopyEdit

routes:

 - name: tenant-a-route

   headers:

     X-Tenant-ID:

       - tenant-a

   paths:

     - /api/v1

   service: tenant-a-service

Best Practices:

- Normalize routing patterns across tenants

- Validate routing logic early in the request lifecycle

- Avoid hardcoding — use plugins or dynamic config services

18.2 Handling Multi-Tenant APIs

A multi-tenant API is a single API surface shared across many tenants, where each tenant may have different:

- Permissions

- Rate limits

- Data isolation rules

- Feature flags

Patterns for Multi-Tenant Gateway Design:

1. Single Gateway, Multi-Tenant Awareness:

   - Gateway introspects the request (headers/token) and attaches tenant metadata.

   - Downstream services enforce RBAC and data-level isolation.

2. Per-Tenant Gateway Instances (less common):

   - Each tenant gets a separate route, service, or even container.

   - Higher resource cost but useful for high-stakes isolation (e.g., fintech clients).

3. Hybrid:

   - Shared control plane with per-tenant routing logic.

    ○   Config driven by tenant registry stored in Redis, Postgres, or config DB.

Security Implication:

- Always validate the tenant context against the authenticated identity.

- Don't rely solely on headers for tenant identification — cross-check with signed tokens or backend lookups.

18.3 Per-Tenant Rate Limits and Quotas

Different tenants may have different usage plans — free tier, pro, enterprise — each with its own:

- Request rate

- Concurrent connections

- Data volume or bandwidth limits

API gateways can enforce per-tenant rate limiting using request metadata (headers, JWT claims, API keys).

Implementation Examples:

Kong Rate-Limiting Plugin:

yaml

```
config:
  minute: 1000
  policy: redis
  limit_by: header
  header_name: X-Tenant-ID
```

Apigee Quota Policy (per app):

xml

```xml
<Quota name="QuotaPerTenant">
  <Allow count="10000"/>
  <Interval>1</Interval>
  <TimeUnit>day</TimeUnit>
  <Identifier ref="request.header.x-tenant-id"/>
</Quota>
```

Tips:

- Store tenant rate limits in a centralized config store or tenant DB.

- Use caching to reduce overhead from tenant lookups.

- Expose quota usage via response headers or developer portals.

Bonus: Use rate limits to monetize tiers (e.g., $99/month = 100K API calls).

18.4 Role-Based Routing and Custom Plugins

Tenants often have multiple user roles — admins, editors, viewers — and different traffic profiles. Role-based routing allows gateways to adapt behavior dynamically based on who's calling the API.

Scenarios:

- Admins get access to audit APIs; viewers do not.

- Editors get higher concurrency than read-only clients.

- Billing APIs are blocked for third-party apps.

Techniques:

- Extract role from JWT claim: user.role == 'admin'

- Use Kong's PDK or NGINX Lua to write plugins that:

    - Route based on roles

    - Enforce role-specific headers or limits

    - Transform responses (e.g., redacted for viewers)

Sample Lua Snippet (OpenResty):

lua
CopyEdit

```
local jwt = require "resty.jwt"
local token = ngx.var.http_authorization
local decoded = jwt:verify("secret", token)

if decoded.payload.role == "admin" then
  ngx.var.backend = "admin-service"
else
  ngx.var.backend = "user-service"
end
```

Note: These custom plugins should run early (e.g., in access_by_lua) and must be performance-optimized to avoid slowing down requests.

18.5 Real-Life Use Case: SaaS Gateway Design

Context:

A B2B SaaS platform hosts hundreds of tenant applications through a shared API gateway. Tenants range from small startups to large enterprises. Each tenant:

- Has isolated data and roles

- Uses the same base URL structure

- Requires per-tenant billing and usage tracking

Architecture Overview:

- Gateway: Kong in DB-less mode behind AWS ALB

- Tenant Registry: DynamoDB with tenant metadata (limits, roles, routing)

- Identity: OAuth2 (Auth0) issuing tenant-scoped tokens

- Metrics: Prometheus with per-tenant labels

- Billing: Kafka events emitted per request, consumed by billing microservice

Request Flow:

1. Client sends request with:

   o Header: X-Tenant-ID

   o Bearer token: eyJ... with claims { "tenant_id": "abc123", "role": "admin" }

2. Kong Plugin:

   o Verifies token

   o Fetches tenant metadata from cache

   o Applies rate limit and logs usage

- o Forwards to https://internal-api/abc123/orders

3. Logging Plugin:

- o Emits metric and billing event to Kafka

Outcomes:

- Tenants are isolated without duplicated infrastructure

- New tenants are onboarded via config sync — no deploy needed

- Teams have full observability and control per tenant

- The gateway enforces consistent policies across tenants and roles

---

Closing Thoughts on Multi-Tenancy and Dynamic Routing

API gateways play a pivotal role in enabling scalable, secure multi-tenancy. They allow SaaS providers and platform builders to abstract tenant logic from backend services — delivering tenant-aware rate limits, routing, role controls, and usage insights all at the edge.

By leveraging:

- Token- and header-based routing

- Config-driven rate limiting

- Role-sensitive access control

- Custom plugins and tenant registries

…you build an architecture that scales to hundreds (or thousands) of tenants with clean separation, consistent governance, and maximum flexibility.

Chapter 19: Hybrid and Multi-Cloud API Gateway Designs

19.1 Designing for Hybrid Cloud Environments

Hybrid cloud refers to architectures where workloads span both on-premises infrastructure and one or more cloud providers. In such setups, your API gateway must serve as a unified interface — securely connecting and orchestrating requests across fragmented environments.

Challenges in Hybrid API Gateways:

- Inconsistent authentication and access control mechanisms

- Network segmentation and firewalls

- Latency between environments

- Different teams managing on-prem vs cloud APIs

Design Patterns:

1. Centralized Gateway Pattern

    ○ A cloud-hosted gateway proxies all requests (even for on-prem APIs).

    ○ Works well if latency is tolerable and on-prem APIs are exposed via VPN or private interconnect.

2. Decentralized Gateway Pattern

   ○ Deploy separate gateways on-prem and in the cloud.

   ○ Use shared control plane or CI/CD to sync policy and routing logic.

3. Edge Aggregator

   ○ API gateway deployed at the edge (e.g., AWS CloudFront + Lambda@Edge).

   ○ Handles routing to cloud or on-prem based on headers, tenant ID, or path.

Example: Apigee Hybrid

- Control plane in Google Cloud

- Runtime plane in on-prem Kubernetes

- Managed APIs span ERP (on-prem), CRM (cloud), and partner APIs

Best Practices:

- Use a common authentication mechanism (e.g., JWT or mTLS) across environments.

- Abstract routing with logical service names (orders-service), not physical IPs.

- Monitor latency between environments to inform retry/backoff strategy.

19.2 Cross-Cloud Routing and Federation

In multi-cloud environments, services run across two or more public clouds — typically AWS, Azure, and GCP — either by design (vendor independence) or acquisition (multiple cloud-native teams).

Core Objectives:

- Minimize lock-in by keeping API control cloud-agnostic

- Route traffic between clouds securely and intelligently

- Maintain consistent policy enforcement regardless of cloud

Approaches to Cross-Cloud Routing:

1. DNS-Level Federation

    o Use a smart DNS (Route 53, NS1) to direct users based on region or latency.

    o Each cloud has its own API gateway; global DNS routes traffic.

2. Gateway Mesh with Shared Identity

    ○ Each cloud has its own API gateway instance.

    ○ All gateways share a common identity provider (e.g., Auth0, Okta).

    ○ Token introspection and claims are consistent regardless of cloud.

3. Service Interconnect via Tunnels

    ○ Gateways communicate via private interconnects, VPNs, or peering links.

    ○ Secure APIs on Cloud A are callable from Cloud B with mutual TLS.

4. Control Plane Syncing

    ○ Use tools like decK, Terraform, or service meshes (Istio, Consul) to sync gateway configs across clouds.

Tools:

- AWS Transit Gateway

- GCP Interconnect

- Azure Virtual WAN

- HashiCorp Consul Mesh

- Kong Ingress Controller across clusters

Key Consideration: Ensure consistency of authentication, authorization, rate limiting, and observability across clouds.

19.3 Common Pitfalls and Workarounds

While hybrid and multi-cloud gateways offer flexibility, they also introduce operational complexity. Below are common traps and how to address them.

Pitfall #1: Inconsistent Policy Enforcement

- Problem: Different gateway instances enforce different rules or plugin versions.

- Fix: Use GitOps to sync configs across environments. Employ decK, Terraform, or centralized config registries.

Pitfall #2: Latency and Failover Complexity

- Problem: High cross-cloud latency or failover logic too complex to manage.

- Fix: Keep services and their API gateways in the same region. Prefer local fallback over cross-cloud retries.

Pitfall #3: Identity Fragmentation

- Problem: Cloud A uses Cognito, Cloud B uses Azure AD, and on-prem uses LDAP.

- Fix: Adopt a centralized identity broker (Auth0, Okta, or custom OIDC layer) to issue unified JWTs.

Pitfall #4: Cost Overruns

- Problem: Routing traffic unnecessarily between clouds increases egress costs.

- Fix: Apply intelligent routing policies to localize traffic. Use caching/CDNs for static APIs.

Pitfall #5: Observability Silos

- Problem: Each cloud has its own metrics, logging, and tracing system.

- Fix: Standardize on OpenTelemetry or export to a central observability platform like Datadog or New Relic.

19.4 Cloud Interconnect and Secure Tunnel APIs

To enable secure traffic between cloud APIs (or on-prem to cloud), you must bridge network boundaries without exposing services publicly.

Techniques:

1. Private Interconnects

    ○ Direct fiber links between your data center and cloud VPCs (e.g., AWS Direct Connect, Azure ExpressRoute, GCP Interconnect).

    ○ High throughput, low latency, and private IP communication.

2. Site-to-Site VPNs

    ○ Encrypted tunnels over public internet.

    ○ Easier to set up, but lower throughput and potentially higher latency.

3. mTLS + Gateway Exposure

    ○ Public-facing API Gateway only allows authenticated, mTLS-encrypted traffic from specific IPs or certs.

4. Cloud NAT + Reverse Proxy

    ○ One cloud makes outbound calls to another cloud's private endpoint via NAT + gateway forwarding.

Gateway-Specific Features:

- Apigee: Secure VPN or interconnect-based routing

- AWS API Gateway + VPC Link: Securely invoke private NLBs

- NGINX with OpenVPN: Tunnel requests from cloud to on-prem

Best Practices:

- Use zero trust principles: assume breach, validate every request

- Encrypt all cross-cloud traffic using TLS 1.2 or higher

- Avoid static IP dependencies — use service discovery or DNS wherever possible

---

19.5 Case Study: Multi-Cloud Gateway for Enterprise

Scenario:

A global enterprise SaaS provider delivers APIs from AWS (core services), GCP (data analytics), and Azure (regional compliance) — and must offer a seamless experience to developers via a unified API surface.

Architecture:

- Global API Gateway: Kong Gateway deployed in AWS, Azure, and GCP.

- Traffic Distribution: NS1 latency-based routing sends users to the closest region.

- Authentication: Okta provides OIDC tokens valid across all clouds.

- Configuration Management:

- Gateway configs stored in Git

- Each cloud uses a CI/CD runner to sync with its gateway

- Cross-Cloud Communication:

  - AWS ↔ GCP: Interconnect over private link

  - Azure ↔ AWS: VPN tunnel + mTLS between internal load balancers

Routing Logic:

- /api/v1/analytics/* → Forward to GCP backend

- /api/v1/payments/* → AWS services (default)

- /api/v1/compliance/* → Azure region due to local data residency laws

Results:

- 99.99% uptime across clouds

- SLA guarantees per region, not per cloud

- Cost-effective cross-cloud traffic routing (latency + cost optimized)

- Centralized dashboards via Grafana using OpenTelemetry

Closing Thoughts on Multi-Cloud API Gateway Designs

Whether you're operating in a hybrid model, expanding across clouds, or unifying teams post-acquisition, API gateways provide a strategic control layer. But success lies in thoughtful architecture — not just deploying multiple gateways, but ensuring:

- Consistent security policies

- Unified observability

- Flexible, maintainable routing logic

- Secure, private service communication

A well-designed multi-cloud gateway isn't just cloud-agnostic — it's resilient, cost-efficient, and user-centric.

Chapter 20: Scaling for Millions of Requests

20.1 Load Testing and Capacity Planning

Before an API gateway can reliably handle millions of requests, you must first understand its breaking points. That starts with rigorous load testing and structured capacity planning.

Why It Matters:

- Helps prevent sudden outages under peak load

- Reveals resource bottlenecks (CPU, memory, I/O)

- Enables data-driven autoscaling decisions

- Validates performance of rate-limiting, auth, and plugins at scale

Load Testing Tools:

- k6: Modern load testing tool with JS scripting

- Locust: Python-based for behavioral tests

- Artillery: Lightweight and cloud-ready

- JMeter: Legacy but still popular in enterprise

What to Measure:

- Requests per second (RPS) throughput

- Average and P95 latency

- CPU/memory utilization of gateway pods/instances

- Rate-limiter effectiveness under burst loads

- Error rates and plugin impact

Example Test Scenario (k6):

javascript

CopyEdit

```
export default function () {
  http.get('https://api.company.com/orders');
}
```

Best Practices:

- Always simulate real-world traffic patterns

- Run tests pre-deployment and post-changes

- Test with auth, plugins, and downstream services enabled

20.2 Autoscaling Gateways with KEDA and HPA

Handling millions of requests isn't just about brute-force power — it's about elastic infrastructure that scales up and down based on demand.

Kubernetes-Based Autoscaling:

- HPA (Horizontal Pod Autoscaler): Scales pods based on metrics like CPU or memory.

- KEDA (Kubernetes Event-Driven Autoscaling): Scales based on custom metrics or external triggers (e.g., Kafka lag, queue depth, Prometheus alerts).

Example: Autoscale Kong Gateway Pods

yaml

CopyEdit

```
apiVersion: autoscaling/v2beta2
kind: HorizontalPodAutoscaler
metadata:
  name: kong-hpa
spec:
  scaleTargetRef:
    apiVersion: apps/v1
    kind: Deployment
    name: kong
  minReplicas: 3
  maxReplicas: 20
  metrics:
    - type: Resource
      resource:
```

```yaml
    name: cpu
    target:
      type: Utilization
      averageUtilization: 60
```

With KEDA:

Scale based on requests-per-second exported to Prometheus:

yaml

CopyEdit

```yaml
triggers:
 - type: prometheus
   metadata:
     serverAddress: http://prometheus:9090
     metricName: kong_requests_per_second
     threshold: '500'
```

Scaling Tips:

- Pre-warm gateway instances during known traffic spikes

- Use low TTL DNS for fast updates when scaling

- Ensure downstream services (databases, caches) also scale

20.3 Batching, Caching, and Compression

When raw scale isn't enough, efficiency patterns like batching, caching, and compression help reduce backend strain and latency.

Batching:

- Combine multiple small requests into one backend call.

- Example: /batch?calls=[{GET:/user},{GET:/orders}]

- Reduces connection overhead, especially for mobile or IoT.

Note: Implement with care — may increase payload size and complexity.

Caching:

- Use response caching at gateway level or via CDN

- Cache:

    o Read-heavy endpoints (/products, /categories)

    o Auth or profile lookups

- Plugins: Kong Cache, NGINX proxy_cache, Apigee ResponseCache

Compression:

- Gzip or Brotli compress JSON responses

- Reduces payload size by 60–90%

- Implement at gateway layer or backend service

Example (NGINX):

nginx
CopyEdit
gzip on;
gzip_types application/json application/javascript text/css;

Best Practices:

- Respect cache headers (Cache-Control, ETag)

- Compress large responses (>1KB); avoid compressing already-compressed content (e.g., images)

- Use smart cache invalidation via tags or TTLs

20.4 High Availability Considerations

Handling millions of requests isn't just about scaling up — it's about ensuring your system never becomes a single point of failure.

HA Principles:

- Redundancy: Run multiple gateway instances in multiple zones

- Statelessness: Ensure gateways can be restarted or rotated instantly

- Health Checks: Constant probing of gateway and upstream service health

- Traffic Routing: Use load balancers with failover rules

Techniques:

- Multi-Zone Deployment:

  - Kubernetes pods distributed across AZs

  - Gateway behind cross-zone load balancer

- Active-Active Configs:

  - Run gateway clusters in parallel (e.g., US-East and US-West)

- Distributed Rate Limiting:

  - Use Redis or Cassandra to synchronize counters

  - Avoid in-memory-only limits in HA setups

Tooling:

- AWS ALB/NLB

- GCP Cloud Load Balancing

- NGINX with Keepalived for on-prem

- Consul for service discovery

Disaster Recovery Tip:
Keep infrastructure-as-code snapshots to rehydrate your entire API layer from scratch in another region or cloud if needed.

20.5 Real-World Scaling Stories: From Startup to Unicorn

Case Study 1: Startup on Kong with 50 RPS

- Began with a single Kong container

- Hit limits during a product launch event

- Migrated to Kubernetes + HPA

- Added Redis-backed rate limiting + OpenTelemetry for tracing

- Now runs 50+ gateway pods across 3 regions

Lesson: Start simple, but invest early in metrics and config management.

Case Study 2: Fintech App at 5,000 RPS

- API Gateway: AWS API Gateway (HTTP + WebSocket)

- Integrated with Lambda backend and Cognito for auth

- Spent time optimizing cache TTLs and enabling gzip

- Scaled vertically (provisioned throughput) + horizontally (multiple endpoints)

Lesson: With serverless gateways, cost is a function of design — optimize routes and caching.

Case Study 3: Enterprise with 100M Daily Requests

- Multi-region Kong clusters (US, EU, APAC)

- Route 53 latency routing

- decK + GitHub Actions for config sync

- Per-tenant rate limits and observability

- Chaos testing used to verify scaling under simulated outage

Lesson: Scaling is not just traffic — it's configuration hygiene, resilience, and trust in automation.

Closing Thoughts on Scaling for Millions of Requests

Scalability isn't just about adding more pods or CPUs. It's about:

- Designing for elasticity

- Observing and reacting to pressure

- Optimizing efficiency (batching, caching, compression)

- Failing gracefully and recovering fast

When done right, your API gateway becomes a performance enabler, not a bottleneck — giving your platform the headroom to grow from startup to unicorn to global leader.

Appendices

Appendix A: API Gateway Comparison Matrix

A well-informed decision between API gateways depends on nuanced differences in capabilities, cost, extensibility, and cloud integration. The table below compares major API gateway solutions across core feature categories.

Feature Comparison: AWS API Gateway vs Azure APIM vs GCP Apigee vs Kong vs NGINX

Feature	AWS API Gateway	Azure API Management	GCP Apigee	Kong Gateway	NGINX/OpenResty
Deployment Model	Fully managed	Fully managed / Hybrid	Fully managed / Hybrid	Self-hosted / Hybrid	Self-hosted
Protocol Support	REST, HTTP, WebSocket	REST, SOAP, WebSocket	REST, GraphQL	REST, gRPC	REST, WebSocket
Rate Limiting	Built-in	Policy-based	Policy-based	Plugin-based	Lua scripting
Authentication	IAM, Cognito, JWT	OAuth2, JWT,	OAuth2, JWT	OAuth2, JWT, HMAC	External or scripted

		Subscription Keys			
Custom Plugins	Limited (Lambda)	No	Limited	Yes (Lua, Go)	Yes (Lua)
Multi-Tenant Support	API keys, claims	Subscription models	Developer portals	Header or JWT routing	Manual config
Observability	CloudWatch	Azure Monitor	Stackdriver, OpenTelemetry	Prometheus, OTel	Prometheus, Fluentd
CI/CD Integration	SAM, CDK	ARM/Bicep, DevOps	gcloud, Terraform	decK, Terraform	Helm, Ansible
Cost Model	Pay-per-call	Instance-based	Subscription tiers	BYOL / Open Source	BYOL / Open Source
Best Suited For	Serverless workloads	Enterprise integration	Global API mesh	Cloud-native platforms	Performance tuning

Tip: Choose based on organizational maturity. Startups may favor Kong or AWS; enterprises often align with Apigee or Azure.

Appendix B: CI/CD Pipeline Templates

Automating API gateway deployments ensures consistency, reduces human error, and accelerates release cycles.

GitHub Actions Workflow for Kong (decK)
yaml
CopyEdit

```
name: Deploy Kong Config

on:
  push:
    branches: [ main ]
    paths:
      - kong/kong.yaml

jobs:
  deploy:
    runs-on: ubuntu-latest
    steps:
      - name: Checkout Code
        uses: actions/checkout@v2

      - name: Set up decK
        run: |
          curl -Lo deck
https://github.com/kong/deck/releases/latest/download/deck-linux-amd64
          chmod +x deck
          sudo mv deck /usr/local/bin
```

- name: Deploy Config
    run: deck sync --state kong/kong.yaml --headers kong-admin-token:${{
secrets.KONG_ADMIN_TOKEN }}

Terraform Template for AWS API Gateway + Lambda

hcl

CopyEdit

```
resource "aws_api_gateway_rest_api" "my_api" {
  name        = "example-api"
  description = "Example API Gateway with Lambda Integration"
}

resource "aws_lambda_function" "api_handler" {
  function_name = "exampleLambda"
  handler       = "index.handler"
  runtime       = "nodejs18.x"
  # code details...
}

resource "aws_api_gateway_integration" "lambda_integration" {
  rest_api               = aws_api_gateway_rest_api.my_api.id
  resource_id            = aws_api_gateway_resource.api_resource.id
  http_method            = aws_api_gateway_method.api_method.http_method
  integration_http_method = "POST"
  type                   = "AWS_PROXY"
  uri                    = aws_lambda_function.api_handler.invoke_arn
}
```

263

Kubernetes Manifests for Gateway Deployment (Kong Ingress Controller)

yaml

CopyEdit

```yaml
apiVersion: apps/v1
kind: Deployment
metadata:
  name: kong
spec:
  replicas: 2
  selector:
    matchLabels:
      app: kong
  template:
    metadata:
      labels:
        app: kong
    spec:
      containers:
        - name: proxy
          image: kong/kong-gateway:latest
          env:
            - name: KONG_DATABASE
              value: "off"
            - name: KONG_DECLARATIVE_CONFIG
              value: /kong/kong.yaml
          volumeMounts:
            - name: config-volume
              mountPath: /kong
```

```
volumes:
  - name: config-volume
    configMap:
      name: kong-config
```

Appendix C: OpenAPI and Swagger Integration

API specification-driven development is critical for consistent contract design, documentation, and automated configuration.

Documenting APIs for Gateway Consumption

Using OpenAPI 3.0:

yaml
CopyEdit
```
openapi: 3.0.0
info:
  title: Order API
  version: 1.0.0
paths:
  /orders:
    get:
      summary: Get Orders
      responses:
        '200':
          description: OK
```

Use tools like:

- Swagger Editor to build specs visually

- Redoc for styled documentation

- OpenAPI Generator for SDK scaffolding

Automating Gateway Config from Specs

Many gateways support auto-generating routes and services directly from OpenAPI specs.

Examples:

- Kong: Use konnect-openapi-importer

- AWS API Gateway: Use aws apigateway import-rest-api

- Apigee: Upload OpenAPI spec via Apigee UI or gcloud CLI

Sample CLI (AWS):

bash
CopyEdit

```
aws apigateway import-rest-api \
  --parameters endpointConfigurationTypes=REGIONAL \
  --body 'file://openapi.yaml'
```

Appendix D: Gateway Design Checklists

To ensure consistency, security, and resilience, use the following practical checklists when launching or auditing your API gateway.

Security Hardening Checklist

- ■ All traffic encrypted (HTTPS, TLS 1.2+)
- ■ Mutual TLS enabled for internal service calls
- ■ JWT/OAuth2 enforced for all protected routes
- ■ No hardcoded secrets — use secret managers
- ■ Rate limiting configured for all public routes
- ■ CORS and HTTP headers (e.g., X-Frame-Options) correctly set
- ■ API keys and tokens rotated periodically
- ■ Audit logging enabled (access + auth events)
- ■ Gateway admin interface IP-restricted
- ■ Default admin credentials changed or disabled

Deployment and Operations Checklist

- ■ Gateway is stateless and horizontally scalable
- ■ Config stored in Git (GitOps)
- ■ CI/CD pipeline in place for gateway updates
- ■ Readiness/liveness probes defined
- ■ Gateway versioning tested on staging
- ■ Failover and timeout settings validated

- Observability stack integrated (logs, metrics, traces)
- Canary deployments supported
- Disaster recovery playbooks tested quarterly

Closing Note on Appendices

These appendices serve as a practical toolkit — designed to accelerate implementation, reduce decision friction, and ensure your architecture aligns with real-world reliability, security, and scalability standards. Whether you're deploying your first gateway or managing thousands of routes across regions, the materials here will help guide your way forward.